FUNDAMENTALS
of
Intellectual Property Rights

I0480124

FUNDAMENTALS
of
Intellectual Property Rights

For Students, Industrialist and Patent Lawyers

Ramakrishna B & Anil Kumar H.S

Notion Press

Old No. 38, New No. 6
McNichols Road, Chetpet
Chennai - 600 031

First Published by Notion Press 2017
Copyright © Ramakrishna B & Anil Kumar H.S 2017
All Rights Reserved.

ISBN 978-1-946556-31-8

Dedicated to

"The soul that ignited the spirit of learning amongst the youth"

Dr. A.P.J Abdul Kalam

Contents

1. **Introduction to Intellectual Property Rights(IPR)** 1

   1.1: Historical Prospective of IPR 1

   1.2: Invention and Creativity 4

   1.3: Importance and Need for Protection of Intellectual Property (IP) 7

   1.4: Emerging Trends in IPR 7

2. **Basic Forms of Intellectual Property Rights** 11

   2.1: Introduction to Basic Forms of Intellectual Property Rights 11

   2.2: Copyright and Neighbouring Laws 16

   2.3: Trade Mark, Trade Name, Service Marks and Trade Secret 20

   2.4: Industrial Design 25

   2.5: Layout Designs of Integrated Circuits 29

   2.6: Geographical Indication (GI) 31

   2.7: Emerging Forms-Traditional Knowledge and Domain Name 33

3. **Patents** 43

   3.1: Introduction to Patent and Types of Patent Applications 43

   3.2: Patent Specifications 51

   3.3: Patent Filing and Examinations 53

   3.4: Patent Search and Databases 62

   3.5: Commercializing Patent Technology 64

4. **Agreements and Treaties** 69

   4.1: General Agreement on Trade and Tariff (GATT) 69

   4.2: Trade Related Aspects of Intellectual Property Rights (TRIPS) 71

   4.3: World Trade Organization 77

   4.4: World Intellectual Property Organization WIPO 88

   4.5: Madrid System 91

4.6: Hague Agreement...94

4.7: The Berne Convention for the Protection of Literary and Artistic Works, 1886...............96

4.8: Paris Convention for the Protection of Industrial Property...103

4.9: Budapest Treaty 107

5. Case studies **117**

5.1: Turmeric Patent Case...117

5.2: Basmati Rice Case 118

5.3: Ginger Case...119

5.4: Bajaj Auto Limited vs. TVS Motor Company Limited Case...120

5.5: The Coca-Cola Company vs. Bisleri International Pvt. Ltd Case 121

5.6: Apple vs Samsung Case 121

Model Questions.. *125*

Introduction to Intellectual Property Rights(IPR)

1

1.1: Historical Prospective of IPR

Intellectual Property Rights (IPRs) became economically and politically very important for both the developed and developing countries after the Agreement on *Trade Related Aspects of Intellectual Property Rights* (TRIPs) were concluded during the Uruguay Round of negotiations of UNO in 1994. This agreement incorporated IPRs into the multilateral trading system. Since then, their relationship with a wide range of public policy issues has elicited great concern over their pervasive role in people's lives and in society in general. They are frequently mentioned in discussions and debates on topics as diverse as education, health, trade, industrial policy, traditional knowledge, IT and media industries.

Intellectual Property Rights(IPRs) refers to the creation of human intellect. These could be ideas or expressions or devices. The WIPO (*World Intellectual Property Organization*) provides further clarification on what exactly should be nature of Intellectual Property. As per the convention, establishing the WIPO, 'intellectual property' includes rights relating to:

- Inventions in all fields of human endeavours,
- Scientific discoveries,
- Industrial designs,
- Trade marks, Service marks and commercial names and designations,
- Literary, artistic and scientific works,
- Performances of performing artists, phonograms, broadcasts,
- Protection against unfair competition; and all other rights resulting from intellectual activity in the industrial, scientific, literary or artistic fields.

The concept of intellectual property goes back to very ancient times. Authors complained about the theft of their work in the Greek and Roman times. 'Potter's marks' were recognized more than 2,000 years ago in Rome as distinguishing marks of the producer. Legal protection for intellectual property goes back to the Middle Ages. In the fifteenth century, Venice has a law protecting patents. In 1449, a patent was granted for the glass making process in England. After the invention of printing with movable typefaces by Guttenberg, many countries of Europe, including England, introduced legal restrictions on printing, which led to the emergence of modern copyright legislation.

The Statute of Anne in 1709 is known as the mother of all copyright laws. In modern jurisprudence, the emergence of international harmonized laws on intellectual property can be traced to the Paris Convention for the Protection of Industrial Property (1883) [*The Paris Convention, concluded in 1883, was revised at Brussels in 1900, at Washington in 1911, at The Hague in 1925, at London in 1934, at Lisbon in 1958 and at*

Stockholm in 1967, and it was amended in 1979] and the Berne Convention for the Protection of Literary and Artistic Works of 1886.

Various developments in the field of IPRs over the years throughout the world including India associated with International Agreements, Treaties, Conventions on IPRs (such as General Agreement on Trade and Tariff (GATT), Trade Related Intellectual Property Rights (TRIPs), Madrid Agreement, Hague Agreement, WIPO (World Intellectual Property Organization), Budapest Treaty, PCT (Patent Cooperation Treaty) agreements, WTO agreement, and many more. The roots of the modern patent regime can be traced in the Venetian System, the British and American System.

History of Intellectual Property Rights (IPRs) in India:

In India in 1856, the first patent system was introduced. In 1859, special privilege exclusively for the inventor was established which conferred the sole use and selling of the creator's or originator's invention for 14 years. This act was replaced by Invention & Designs Act, 1888; which was once again repeated by Indian Patents and Designs Act, 1911. In 1930, there were some major amendments in the similar act. In 1948, the Government of India appointed a Patents Enquiry Committee under Dr. Tek Chand, and the committee submitted its report in 1953 but this bill lapsed due to dissolution of Lok Sabha.

In late 1950s, when political and economic set up was being enhanced the Indian pharmaceutical industry was being dominated by the foreign multinational companies. The prices of the drugs with special mention to life saving drugs were too high. These prices were non-affordable by the common people in India. The previous acts were not being able to meet the needs and aspirations of a newly independent nation and observing such chaos in the pharmaceutical sector the Indian Government in 1957 appointed a committee under the Chairmanship of Justice Raja Ayyangar. The committee started its work keeping in mind the changing scenario. The report was inspired by the Indian Constitution which ensures social and economic justice. Article 21 of the Indian Constitution which ensures the right to health to citizens was the guiding philosophy behind Ayyangar committee recommendations. This led to the structure for the 'Process Patenting' in India. This report was submitted in Lok Sabha in 1966.

The history of IPR legislations in India with respect to various IPR protection forms:

Patents: Chronologically

1856	The Act VI of 1856 on protection of inventions based on the British Patent Law offered certain exclusive privileges granted to inventions of new manufactures for a period of 14 years
1859	The Act modified as Act XV, patent monopolies called Exclusive privileges
1872	The Patents and Designs Protection Act
1883	The Protection of Inventions Act
1888	Consolidated as Inventions Act
1911	The Indian Patents and Designs Act
1970	The Patents Act
1972	The Patents Act (Act 39 of 1970) came into force on 20th April 1972
1999	A bill of comprehensive amendment of Patents Act, 1970 was introduced in Lok Sabha

| 2002 | The above bill was passed on 8th May, 2002 as Patents (Amendment) Act and came into force on 20th May 2003 |

2002   The above bill was passed on 8th May, 2002 as Patents (Amendment) Act and came into force on 20th May 2003

2005   The Patents Act, 1970 as amended by the Patents (Amendments) Act, 2005 alsong with the Patents (Amendments) Rules, 2005 (w.e.f 1st January 2005)

The Patents Act 1970 (which came into effect in 1972) removed Product Patent from three sectors, namely Pharmaceuticals, Food and Agrochemicals. On the remaining sectors, Product Patent continued on par with other countries worldwide including USA and UK.

Once pharmaceuticals were removed from the shackles of the Product Patent, the growth of the indigenous Pharmaceutical industry was swift. It grew from a scratch in 1947 and a tiny industry in 1970 to a respectable level of Rs.70,000 Crores plus industry (including Pharma Exports worth Rs.30,000 Crores) now.

The Patents Act (Act 39 of 1970) came into force on 20th April 1972. The Patents Act of 1970 was designed perfectly in tune with our then national ideology of planned development. This was the time when there was socialistic planning. Since then India has underwent an absolute economic enhancement. India has taken up the strands of globalization and liberalization. Today the country is gaining momentum ahead of the global economy. This process will not be complete unless the research and development is also integrated with global research and development. Also India has entered into an international framework after being the member of WTO. Thus, it is in the legal obligation to fulfill all the statutory norms of the WTO. To satisfy the statutory norms of the TRIPS agreements, India is conditionally updating its patent regime.

Designs:

The Designs Act, 2000 along with The Designs Rules, 2001 has been implements over and above the earlier Designs Act, 1911.

Trademark: Chronologically:

1958   The Trade and Merchandise Marks Act

1999   The Trade Marks Act, 1999 came into force from September 15, 2003

2002   The Trade Marks Rules Act.

Copyright: Chronologically:

1957   The Copyright Act, 1957

1958   The Copyright Rules Act, 1958

1983   The Copyright (Amendment) Act, 1983

1984   The Copyright (Amendment) Act, 1984

1992   The Copyright (Amendment) Act, 1992

1994   The Copyright (Amendment) Act, 1994

1999   The Copyright (Amendment) Act, 1999 (effective from 15th January 2000)

Layout Design of Integrated Circuits:

The Semiconductor Integrated Circuit Layout Design Act, 2000 (enforcement pending)

***Protection of Undisclosed Information (Trade Secrets)*:**

No exclusive legislation exists, but the matter would be generally covered under the Contract Act, 1872.

***Geographical Indications*:** Chronologically

| 1999 | The Geographical Indications of Goods (Registration and Protection) Act, 1999 |
| 2002 | The Geographical Indications of Goods (Registration and Protection) Act, 2002 |

As the law governing the grant of all these intellectual properties vary form country to country and there are efforts to harmonize Intellectual Property (IP) laws and procedures or to establish minimum standard for IP protection. These efforts are reflected in the international treaties and conventions like Paris Convention, Patent Cooperation Treaty (PCT), and TRIPS, which have been ratified by most of the countries.

1.2: Invention and Creativity

Creativity is the ability to produce new and useful ideas through the combination of known principles and components in novel and non-obvious ways.

In other words, creativity is "playing with imagination and possibilities, leading to new and meaningful connections and outcomes while interacting with ideas, people, and the environment." Creativity exists throughout the population, largely independent of age, sex, and education. Yet in any group a few individual will display creativity completely out of proportion to their number. To have an effective research the organization requires understanding the creative process, identifying and acquiring creative people, and maintaining an environment that supports rather than inhibits creativity.

When it comes to the explanation of **invention** – "it is a new product or process involving an inventive step and capable of industrial application." Inventions grouped into **four statutory classes**:

- Processes
- Machines
- Articles of Manufacture
- Composition of Matter

In patent jargon, an invention is generally defined as **a new and inventive solution to a technical problem**. It may relate to the creation of an entirely new device, product, method or process, or my simply be **an incremental improvement** to a known product or process. Merely finding something that already exists in nature generally doesn't qualify as an invention; an adequate amount of human ingenuity, creativity and inventiveness must be involved. **Most of the inventions nowadays are the result of considerable efforts and long-term investments in Research and Development (R&D)**, may simple and inexpensive technical improvements, of great market value, have yielded significant income and profits to their inventors or companies.

Invention Vs. Innovation:

Appreciating the distinction between 'invention' and 'innovation' is important. Invention refers as we already know to a technical solution to a technical problem. It may be an innovative idea or may be in the form of a working model or prototype. Innovation, on the other hand, refers to the translation of the invention into a marketable product or process. Some of the reasons why the companies innovate include:

1. To improve manufacturing processes in order to save costs and improve productivity.

2. To introduce new products that meet customers' needs.

3. To remain ahead of the competition and/or expand market share.

4. To ensure that technology is developed to meet actual and emerging needs of the business and its clients.

5. To prevent technological dependence on other companies' technology.

In today's business environment, managing innovation within a company requires a good knowledge of the Intellectual Property Rights (IPRs) and protections in order to ensure that the company draws maximum benefit from its own innovative and creative capacity, establishes profitable partnerships with other patent holders and avoid making unauthorized use of technology owned by others. Unlike the past, many innovations nowadays are complex and are based on a number of patented inventions, which may be owned by different patent owners.

The Process of Creativity and Invention:

There are a number of models for problem solving such as – trial and error method, planning/decision-making process – which involves problem definition, identification of alternatives, evaluating them against objectives. Its major thrust is analytical reasoning, although its success is enhanced by some creativity in selection of alternatives to be evaluated. Following are the steps identified in creative and inventive process:

1. **Preparation** – Shannon describes this step as "a period of conscious, direct mental effort devoted to the accumulation of information pertinent to the problem ....and include the areas like:

   a) Structure the problem,

   b) Collect all available information,

   c) Understand relations and effects,

   d) Solve sub-problems; and

   e) Explore all possible solution and combinations that may lead to a satisfactory solution.

2. **Frustration and incubation** – Failure to solve the problem satisfactorily by the analytical process above lead to frustration and the decision to set if aside and get on with something else. However, the problem, fortified with all the facts gathered about it, "stews" or incubates in the subconscious mind.

3. **Inspiration or illumination** – A possible solution to the problem may occur as a spontaneous insight, often when the conscious mind is at rest during relaxation or sleep. Many creative individuals are never without a notepad and pen, on their person or beside table, to write down these flashes of insight.

4. **Verification** – Intuition or insight is not always correct, and the solution revealed in a flash of insight must now be tested and evaluated to assure it is, indeed, a satisfactory solution to the problem.

Shannon defends this model as "...............*When applied to problem solving, the human mind has two aspects:*

1. *a judicial, logical, conscious mind that analyses, compares, and chooses; and*

2. *an imaginative, creative, sub-conscious mind that visualizes, foresees, and generates ideas from stored knowledge and experience.*"

Invention (the creative process) only produces ideas. They are not useful until they are reduced to practice and use, which is the process of innovation. **Kiddder** provides an excellent study of motivation and creativity in the development of a 32-bit computer at Data General. **Roberts** and **Wainer** have identified five kinds of people who are needed for technological innovation:

i. *Idea generator – the creative individual*

ii. *Entrepreneur – the person who "caries the ball"*

iii. *Gatekeeper – high technical performers*

iv. *Program manager – who manage without inhibiting*

v. *Sponsor or Champion – the person, often in senior management, who provides financial and moral support*

Strategic planning for competition implies searching for means of capturing a sustainable advantage. R&D is conducted to develop and improve technological products and processes that provide the organization a competitive advantage. If these advantages are readily duplicated by others, then there is an often insufficient reason for expending the initial resources for a short-term advantage. Therefore, the products and services that have high creative value added content, it is vital to the economic well-being of the creative organizations and countries that there be some means for protection of these intellectual properties. Fortunately, there are means for protection of ideas in all industrialized countries of the world and are popularly called as *"Intellectual Property Rights."*

Intellectual Property (Jurisprudential Definition)

The question here to analyze is what exactly the meaning of a property? The answer to this question associated with the features of the concept of property. The most important and unique feature of any property is that the proprietor or the owner may use the property as he wishes and that nobody else can lawfully use his property without his authorization. This is the legal provision as an exclusive right of the owner to use his property. Naturally the owner is free to authorize others to use his property. Such authorization is legally necessary and the use without the owner's authorization would be illegal.

The general classification of the property involves:

1. Movable property,

2. Immovable property; and

3. Intellectual property.

Property consists of movable things money, jewels, automobiles, and so on. Immovable property includes land and building which is permanently fixed. As far as immovable property is concern certain limits are imposed on the owner's privilege of using such properties. The owner has to respect the applicable legal requirements and administrative formalities as far as the use of immovable property. For example, construction of building on a piece of land bound to follow the legal requirements. Intellectual property is the creation of the human mind, the human intellect and hence called *"intellectual property."* Intellectual property is a critical personal or company asset, as such; it can be bought, sold, mortgaged, licensed, exchanged or gratuitously given away like any other form of the property. Moreover, by acquiring a legal right over the property; the creator of the intellectual property seeks to ensure that he has exclusive right over it and that the property can be put to use by others only with his consent.

Ownership of the Intellectual Property is a source of personal, organizational and national wealth and mark of an economic leadership in the context of the global market scenario.

1.3: Importance and Need for Protection of Intellectual Property (IP)

Any property has to be protected in order to save it from an unauthorized use. At the same time, the Intellectual Property Rights must also be protected from infringement. The rationale for the protection of IP are Intellectual Property Rights (IPRs) related to new ideas, new technology, new products and evolution of knowledge.

Like movable and immovable properties, intellectual property is also the result of effort by one or more human beings, with or without using equipments or machines. Therefore, like the producers of the two other forms of property, the creators of intellectual property also have the right to insist on payment for the product of their labour or for the labour itself. Remuneration for creators of intellectual property became economically significant when cheap, multiple copies of a work could be made and it made sense for the creator to be rewarded for his/her intellectual effort and be protected from potential free riders.

1. In today's knowledge based socio-economic environment, IPRs are key elements needed to maintain the competitive of any industry and nation at large. IPRs impart success to the business enterprise by creating and preserving exclusive markets.

2. The cost of R&D in developing new products and new processes is rising sharply and hence, there is a need to increase and accelerate the extent of protection of IPRs to get reasonable return on investment and reduce the element of risk and uncertainty.

3. IPR protection provides an incentive to inventors for further research and investment in R & D, which leads to creation of new and better products and in turn, brings about economic growth and social benefits.

4. Intellectual properties are emerging as a new knowledge and ideas, have become significant components of world trade.

5. In today's knowledge based socio-economic system, an understating of IPRs is indispensable to informed policy making in all areas of human and national developments.

6. IPR protection helps in harnessing the intellect of the man in developing the human resource and enhances the intellectual capacity of the human beings.

7. IPRs provide the power to build the intellectual property as an important asset of an organization and nation at large.

1.4: Emerging Trends in IPR

Having financial significance, IP has emerged as a substantial tool to overcome the economic crises not only for the under-developed or developing nations but also for developed countries. As firms streamline operations to save money amid the recession, an increased trend of generating cash by selling or licensing dormant trademarks and patents has been observed in these times of global meltdown. Neglected trademarks and patents that have been collecting dust in India, the United States, the United Kingdom, Germany, Japan, China, Brazil and Dubai, where vital information such as intellectual property originates, may turn a new leaf.

There is an opportunity in the cast-off intellectual property for entrepreneurial firms because it can provide a shortcut to success. The small and medium sized enterprises (SMEs), aiming to sustain their existence in the market by challenging the giants, should nullify their size disadvantages by either in-licensing or merger and acquisition. Such a strategy will result in optimum utilization of each other's resources and cutting down the overall risk. However, the innovative and creative capacity, is not always fully exploited because of ignorance of the emerging market trends. With SMEs being the driving forces behind business activities in a nation, they need to take part in technology transfer and innovation. Linkages between SMEs and other enterprises to promote technology transfer would expand consumption markets, as well as improve competitiveness of SMEs.

The available information on important IP issues for SMEs – which takes into account their special needs such as resource constraints, actual knowledge and simpler "business" language – is still limited. IP's potential to overcome the economic crises is restricted by certain limitations in its creation and production, resulting in an imbalance between its demand and supply. Thus, many SMEs are challenged by the peculiarities of the IP system. To help SMEs more fully utilize the emerging trends in their business activities, they need to know more about them. The best resources for updates on the market can be obtained from various sources of reference. Many SME owners take their intellectual property for granted ignoring the worth of it. The first step towards success is to identify the IP rights of one's own company – a brand, slogan, product name, consumer association, product packaging or even a colour scheme – and optimize it to intensify the company's growth.

The Confederation of Indian Industry began organizing the International Conference on IP Laws and Enforcement of IPR from 2014. The first international conference was organized in partnership with Department of Industrial Policy and Promotion (DIPP) as well as Intellectual Property Office (IPO) from 20–21 November 2014. The event featured eminent experts and IP professionals from India and abroad, as well as eminent personalities from Industry, academia, government, R&D institutions and legal luminaries. It was an international event that brought together discerning audiences and eminent speakers to discuss and evolve emerging aspects of intellectual property.

This conference generated much interest among the participants and stakeholders who for the first time experienced a platform so comprehensive and focused for the cause of building the intellectual property ecosystem in the country. The summit brought together the best speakers and thinkers in the domain of IPR from across the world to deliberate on various issues of concern in this domain and the way Forward. (confederation of Indian Industry Annual report 2014–15)

Indian scenario

As in many other developing nations, introduction of TRIPS compatible IP regime has generated a lot of debate in India. In general, the debate has focused more on pharmaceutical and food sectors as these affect access to food and healthcare, two of the most critical human needs. The case of India is different from many other countries given its capabilities in the pharmaceutical industry. The data on health related innovations is fragmented and sketchy and therefore it is not easy to unequivocally answer the question if the new IP regime has fostered inventive and innovative activity in the Indian healthcare sector. The Indian pharmaceutical firms have shown a higher propensity to invent and patent although their R&D focus may have shifted somewhat in favour of Western markets. While there is also a shift in favour of product inventions, not many of these are new chemical entities but new dosage forms and drug delivery mechanisms. There is a lot of activity in the medical devices domain although it is not clear to what extent it has been impacted by the new IP regime. Strategic forays into foreign nations to acquire technology and consolidation in the domestic market seems to be a pre-requisite for Indian firms to deal with the increasing technology based competition. And Indian firms have been quite active on that front. Recent decline in PCT applications is puzzling and needs to be explored. The emergence of IP based start-ups and social ventures in the healthcare space are noteworthy. Given the penetration of the Internet and mobile technologies, supporting such initiatives is critical for healthcare access in the near future. Apart from policy innovations to enhance access and affordability of healthcare services, public policy will need to be flexible to nurture and encourage such experiments. Such flexibility is critical as the success of these ventures is intricately linked to the ability of the start-ups to get integrated with the public healthcare delivery system. Therein lies the essential complementarity between entrepreneurial efforts and public policy innovations. Encouragement of entrepreneurship in the sector requires a combination of powerful financial incentives, capacity for quality research, supportive regulatory system, and an active investment community (FICCI, 2011).

As India gains more experience with the new patent regime, it will have to be cognizant of the dysfunctionalities that the new regime might have created. While the MNCs have complained about the criteria of patentability (Article 3 (d)) and compulsory licensing (Article 84), some small firms seem to have suffered with respect to the confusion regarding the validity of the patents granted (Section 13 (4)). A critical review of these seems desirable. The complaints regarding cumbersome patenting procedures seem to be common across different types of firms. Admittedly, it is a learning phase for the country and the State should be flexible enough to change policy to balance the twin objectives of creating incentives for invention and providing affordable healthcare.(M.D Nair, JIPR, 2010)

Future trend

Global scenario in technology transfer indicates that the world is poised for new and breakthrough innovations in the environment and health care areas, in view of current energy reality and environmental challenges such as global warming. There may be considerable challenges or even opposition to the new options or concepts due to costs or practicality of the innovations. Radical innovation often involves considerable change in basic technologies and methods, created by those working outside existing paradigms. In the past, it has been observed that the rate of patent filing is directly proportional to the economic status of a nation – that is, with a dip in the economic status, the number of patent filings too declines. However, historically, economic crises have also acted as a catalyst for innovation, as greater 26 emphasis is placed on improving standards of efficiency, doing more with less, and identifying and developing smarter business solutions. When the economy recovers, there is improvement also in the patenting activity. In the current economic climate, technology, innovation and creativity are critical in generating opportunities for economic renewal and addressing pressing global issues such as climate change.(Shriya, TECH MONITOR Mar-Apr 2009)

Basic Forms of Intellectual Property Rights 2

2.1: Introduction to Basic Forms of Intellectual Property Rights

The basic types of Intellectual Property Rights are:

- Patent Rights
- Copyrights
- Trade Marks
- Trade Secrets (protection of undisclosed information)
- Industrial Designs
- Geographical Indications
- Design of Integrated Circuit Layouts (Topography of Intergrated Circuits)
- Plant Varieties
- Traditional Knowledge,
- Domain Name, etc.

The Patent rights, Copyrights, Trademarks, Design Patents and Trade Secrets are the commonly used forms of Intellectual Property Rights (IPRs).

Figure: Intellectual Property and its Facets

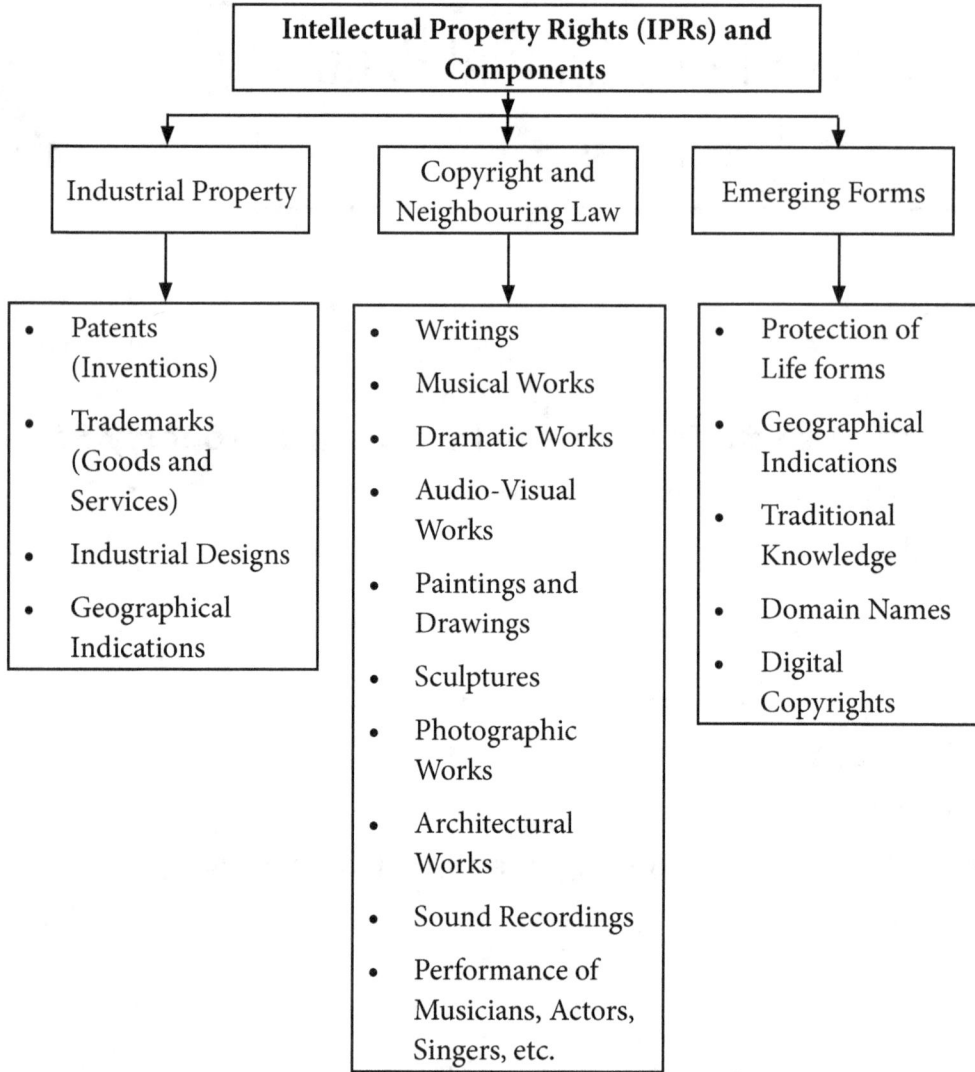

Patent Rights:

The term 'Patent' has its origin in the Latin term "***Litterae Patentes***." The expression meant open letter as distinguished from closed letter. It means a grant of some privilege, property or authority made by the government or the sovereign authority of the country to one or more individuals. The instrument by which such grant is made is known as "Pantent."

What is a Patent?

A patent is a monopoly right to the exclusive use of an invention, granted to the inventor or his assignee. To be more specific a patent "is an ***exclusive right*** granted by the State for an ***invention*** that is new, involves an ***inventive step*** and is ***capable of industrial application***." The right is granted only for a limited period called the term of the patent. This right may cease, if not kept alive by payment of renewal fees. The inventor or his assignee has to apply for the invention to the patent office along with his application disclosing the complete invention in the form of complete specification.

This complete specification is published by the patent office immediately on deciding that a patent my be granted. In many countries, this publication takes place even earlier. Thus, patent is an exclusive right for a limited period of time by the government to the patentee (owner of the patent) in exchange of full disclosure of his invention for making, using, selling the patented product or process or authorizing others to do so. The purpose of this system is to encourage inventions by promoting their protection and better facilities to the society. Once published, the copy of the patent specification is available for inspection for the general public.

The patent right **gives the owner the exclusive right to prevent or stop other** from making, using, offering for sale, selling or importing a product or a process, based on the patented invention, without the owner's prior permission. Moreover, a patent is a **territorial right** and limited to the geographical boundary of the relevant country or region.

Copyrights and Neighbouring (Related) Rights:

Copyright according to *Black's Law Dictionary* is the right in literary property as recognized and sanctioned by positive law. An intangible incorporeal right granted to the author or the originator of certain literary or artistic production whereby the invests for a specified period with the sole and exclusive privilege of multiplying copies of the same and publishing and selling them.

Copyright as defined in the *Oxford English Dictionary* is an exclusive right granted by law for a certain term of years to an author, composer, etc., (or to his assignee) to print, publish and sell copies of his original work.

Copyright Act generally give the owner of the copyright the exclusive right to to and to authorize others to reproduce the work in copies or phono records; to prepare derivative works based upon the work; to distribute copies or phono records of the work to the public by sale or other transfer or ownership, or by rental, lease, or lending; to perform the work publicly, in the case of literary, musical, dramatic, and choreographic works, pantomimes, and pictorial graphics, or sculptural works, including the individual images of a motion picture or other audiovisual work; and in the case of sound recordings, to perform the work publicly by means of a digital audio transmission.

Copyright protects '**original works of authorship**' that are fixed in a tangible form of expression. Copyright protects all creations of the human mind whatever their form or merit and regardless of the audience they are destined for. **Protection is generally immediate** and no formal procedure is requiring as long as the piece of work is original.

Neighbouring Rights (Related Rights), also known as rights neighbouring to copyright, were created for three categories of people who are not technical authors, such as performing artists, producers of phonogram's, and those involved in radio and television broadcasting.

Trade Marks (Goods and Services):

A trade mark is a sign capable of distinguishing the goods or services produced or provided by one enterprise from those of other enterprises. A trademark is also termed as industrial property. It provides the **identification marks** to the goods and services at the time of marketing (buying and selling). Trade marks helps the organizations to acquire distinctiveness with respect to its products and services and helps in earning consumers' brand or product loyalty. It is a **distinctive mark to differentiate** between the similar and identical products of different companies. If trademarks used in connections with services, it may be called as '**service marks.**'

Any **distinctive words, letters, numerals, drawings, pictures, shapes, colours, logotypes, labels or combinations used to distinguish goods and services** may be considered a trademark. In some countries, '**advertising slogans**' are also considered trademarks and registered as such at national trademark offices.

In some of the countries registration of less traditional forms of trademarks also allowed, such as **single colours, three-dimensional signs (shapes of products or packaging), audible signs (sounds) or olfactory signs (smells)**. However, many countries have set limits on what can be registered as a trademark, generally only allowing for signs that are visually perceptible or that can be represented graphically.

The trade marks helps the companies to being pivotal in **the branding and marketing strategies, developing product and brand image, to create trust, establishing a loyal clientele, enhancement of companies' goodwill and develop an emotional attachment** and so on.

Trade Secrets (protection of undisclosed information):

Trade Secrets are confidential business information my benefit from trade secret protection as long as: it is not generally known to other dealing with that type of information, it has commercial value because it is secret; and reasonable steps have been taken by its owner to keep it secret (for example, restricting access to such information on a 'need to know' basis, and entering into confidentiality or non-disclosure agreements)

Industrial Designs:

In everyday language, an industrial design generally refers to **a product's overall form and function**. For business, designing a product generally implies developing the **product's functional and aesthetic features** taking into consideration issues such as the product's marketability, the costs of manufacturing or the ease of transport, storage, repair and disposal.

From an intellectual property law perspective, however, **an industrial design refers only to the ornamental or aesthetic aspects of a product** and is distinct from any technical or functional aspects. As a general rule, an industrial design consists of:

- Three-dimensional features, such as the **shape** of a product,
- Two-dimensional features, such as ornamentation, patterns, lines or colour of a product; or
- a combination of one or more of such features.

Thus, industrial design broadly covers the "look and feel" features of the products.

Geographical Indications:

Geographical Indications inform us about a source of a good that has certain qualities associated with it due to the place of its origin. Qualities and characteristics of certain good attributable to some geographical locations and reputable to "as produce of certain region" come under geographical indications. Only associations can apply for geographical indications.

For example, **Darjeeling Tea, Alfanso Mangoes, Havana Cigars, Sherry Wine, Arabian Horses, Mysore Silk, China Silk, Dhaka Muslin, Venetial glass, Coramandal pearls, Basmati Rice, Kolhapuri chappals, Kanjivaram silks**, and so on.

Each geographical reputation was carefully built up and painstakingly maintained by the masters of that region, combining the best of the nature and man, traditionally handed over to the generations to generations over the centuries.

Design of Integrated Circuit Layouts (Topography of Integrated Circuits):

Integrated Circuits are incorporated into all the electronic devices we use today. The layout of the same can be protected and the owner of the same can take advantage of his work in this area. This is a growing industrial field and in several countries, backbone of the national economy. It involves the protection of

I C Layout Design, PCB Layout Design, and also Miniaturization (ensuring functionality and accuracy), etc.

Plant Varieties:

A "plant variety" is a legal term, and recognition of a cultivated plant as a "variety" provides its breeder with some legal protection, so-called plant breeders' rights, depending to some extent on the internal legislation of the signatory countries.

Traditional Knowledge:

Traditional Knowledge (TK), Indigenous Knowledge (IK), and local knowledge generally refer to the matured longstanding traditions and practices of a certain regional, indigenous or local communities. It also encompasses the wisdom, knowledge, and teachings of these communities. In many cases, traditional knowledge has been orally passed for generations from person to person. Some forms of traditional knowledge are expressed through stories, legends, folklore, rituals, songs, and even laws. Other forms of traditional knowledge are often expressed through different means.

Recently, international attention has turned to intellectual property laws to preserve, protect and promote their traditional knowledge. Three broad approaches to protect traditional knowledge have been developed.

- The first emphasizes protecting traditional knowledge as a form of *cultural heritage.*
- The second looks at protection of traditional knowledge as a *collective human right.*
- The third, taken by WTO and WIPO, investigates the use of existing or novel *sue-generis* measures to protect traditional knowledge.

In this context, worth mentioning Indian success in the fight for the revocation of turmeric and basmati patents granted by United States Patents and Trademarks Office (USPTO) and neem patent granted by European Patent Office (EPO). As a sequel to this, in 1999, the Department of Ayurved, Yoga & Naturopathy, Unani, Siddha and Homeopathy (AYUSH), erstwhile Department of Indian System of Medicine and Homeopathy (ISM&M) constituted an inter-disciplinary Task Force, for preparing an approach paper on establishing a Traditional Knowledge Digital Library (TKDL). It is a collaborative project between National Institute of Science Communication and Information Resources (NISCAIR), Council of Scientific and Industrial Research, Ministry of Science & Technology and Department of AYUSH, Ministry of Health and Family Welfare, which being implement at NISCAIR. An inter-disciplinary team of Traditional Medicine (Ayurveda, Unani, Siddha, Yoga) experts, patent examiners, IT experts, scientists and technical officers are involved in creation of TKDL for Indian Systems of Medicine. The project TKDL involves documentation of the knowledge available in public domain on traditional knowledge from the existing literature related to Ayurveda, Unani, and Siddha in digitized format in five international languages – English, German, French, Japanese and Spanish. Traditional Knowledge Resource Classification (TKRC) is an innovative structured classification system for the purpose of systematic arrangements, dissemination and retrieval has been evolved for about 10,500 subgroups against one group in International Patent Classification (IPC).

Domain Name:

The domain name in the online world, just like the trade name in the offline world, serves to identify the good/services provided by the company. To access a website, one requires a web address. This web address comprises of domain names. As the number if Internet users increased, the importance of domain name also increased. People started identifying the domain name with its owner. With the increased use of internet, the businessmen used it not only for advertising and promoting their products, but also for selling them, the principles of trademark, infringement of trademark and passing off are being applied even in the online environment. One of the primary areas is domain names, which has been legal protection equal to that of a trademark.

2.2: Copyright and Neighbouring Laws

Copyright is a right, which is available for creating an original literary, dramatic, musical, artistic work. Cinematographic films including sound track and video films and recordings on discs, tapes, perforated roll or other devices are covered by copyrights. Computer programs and software are covered under literary works and protected in India under copyrights. As per Indian Copyrights Act, the total term of protection for literary work is the **author's life plus sixty years**. For cinematographic films, records, photographs, posthumous publications, anonymous publication, works of government and international agencies the term of protection under Copyright Act is 60 years from the beginning of the calendar year following the year in which the work was published. For broadcasting, the term is 25 years from the beginning of the calendar year following the year in which the broadcast was made.

Copyright provides protection for the expression of an idea and not for the idea itself.

A Computer Program in the Copyright Act has been defined as a set of instructions expressed in words, codes, schemes or any other form, including a machine-readable medium, capable of causing a computer to perform a particular task or achieve a particular result. It is obvious that algorithms, source codes and object codes are covered in this definition. Generally, all copyrightable expressions embodied in a computer program, including screen displays, are being protected under copyright laws.

Rights Conferred by Copyrights:

The Copyright confers following rights explained in several categories:

a) **Statutory rights**: The copyright in a work is a creation of statue. A person owns a copyright because the law recognizes the existence of such a right. The rights, which an author of a work has by virtue of creating the work, are well defined.

b) **Negative Rights**: Author for their own benefit without the consent or the license of the author. It does not confer any positive rights on the author himself.

c) **Multiple Rights**: Copyright is not a single right, but a bundle of rights, which can exist and be exploited independently. The nature of these multiple rights depends upon the categories of works, namely, literary, dramatic and musical works, original artistic works, cinematograph films, and sound recording, etc.

d) **Economic Rights**: The rights conferred on a copyright owner are economic rights because the exploitation of the work by the author by exercising these rights may bring economic benefit. The author may exploit the work himself or license others to exploit any one or more of the rights for a consideration, which may be in the form of royalty, a lump-sum payment.

e) **Moral Rights**: The copyright also confers moral rights on the author. Such rights, though not statutorily defined, are as follows:

- The right to decide whether to publish or not to publish the work, i.e., right of publication.

- The right to claim authorship of a published or exhibited work.

- The right to prevent alteration or other actions that may damage the author's honour or reputation, i.e., the right of integrity.

These moral rights are recognized as "Author's Special Rights."

To be more specific, the Copyright Act generally gives the owner of copyright the exclusive right to do and to authorize others to do the following:

- To reproduce the work in copies or phonorecords.

- To prepare derivative works based upon the work.

- To distribute copies or phonorecords of the work to the public by sale or other transfer of ownership, or by rental, lease, or lending.

- To perform the work publicly, in the case of literary, musical, dramatic, and choreographic works, pantomimes, and motion pictures and other audiovisual works.

- To display the copyrighted work publicly, in the case of literary, musical, dramatic, and choreographic works, pantomimes, and pictorial, graphic or sculptural works, including the individual images of a motion picture or other audiovisual works.

- In the case of sound recordings, to perform the work publicly by means of a digital audio transmission.

These rights enable the author to control the economic use of the work in a number of ways and to receive payment.

Works that are Protected by the Copyright:

Copyright protects "original works of authorship" that are fixed in a tangible form of expression. The fixation need not be directly perceptible so long as it may be communicated with the aid of a machine or device. Copyrightable works include the following categories:

- Literary works

- Musical works, including any accompanying words

- Dramatic works, including any accompanying music

- Pantomimes and choreographic works

- Motion pictures and other audiovisual works

- Sound recordings

- Architectural works, etc.

These categories should be viewed broadly. For example, computer programs and most "compilations" may be registered as "literary works"; maps and architectural plans may be registered as "pictorial, graphic, and sculptural works."

Works that are not protected by the Copyright:

Several categories of material are generally not eligible for copyright protection. These include among others:

- Works that have not fixed in a tangible form of expression (for example, choreographic works that have not been notated, recorded, improvisational speeches or performances that have not been written or recorded).

- Titles, names, short phrases, and slogans; familiar symbols or designs; mere variations of typographic ornamentation, lettering, or colouring, mere listings of ingredients or contents.

- Ideas, procedures, methods, systems, processes, concepts, principles, discoveries, devices, as distinguished from a description, explanation or illustration.

- Works consisting entirely of information that is common property and containing no original authorship (for example, standard calendars, height and weight charts, tape measures and rulers, and list or tables taken from public documents or other common sources).

Classification of Software according to Copyright:

Software copyright law is something that affects anyone who uses a computer and most particularly the business - it is not uncommon for a business to face civil or criminal proceedings for software infringement.

Software copyright is not essentially different from any other sort of copyright. However, there are certain aspects of copyright law that are specific to software, because there are practical differences between software and other things that can be copyrighted such as books, poems, drawings, sculptures, etc.

Copyright law gives a programmer (or to the employer of the programmer) a high degree of control over the program that he or she creates. The copyright protection to the software is concerned, the classification of the software according to the copyright law include the following four broad categories:

1. Commercial Software
2. Shareware
3. Freeware
4. Public Domain

1. Commercial Software:

Commercial software represents the majority of software purchased from software publishers, commercial computer stores, etc. If client or customer buys software, he or she is actually acquiring a license to use it, not own it. The client or customer acquires the license from the company that owns the copyright. The condition and restrictions of the license agreement vary from program to program and should be read carefully. In general, commercial software licenses stipulate that:

- The software is covered by the copyright.

- Although one archival copy of the software can be made, the backup copy cannot be used except when the original package fails or is destroyed.

- A modification to the software is not allowed.

- Decompiling (i.e., reverse engineering) of the program code is not allowed without the permission of the copyright holder; and

- Development of new works built upon the package (derivative works) is not allowed without the permission of the copyright holder.

2. Shareware:

Shareware as a software is covered by copyright. On acquiring of software under a shareware arrangement, the users are actually acquiring a license to use it, not own it. The users acquire the license from the individual or company that owns the copyright.

The conditions and restrictions of the license agreement vary from program to program and should be read carefully. The copyright holders for *shareware* allow purchasers to make and distribute the copies of the software, but demand that if, after resting the software; the users adopt it for use and must pay for it. In general, *shareware*, software license stipulate that:

- The software is covered by the copyright.

- Although one archival copy of the software can be made, the backup copy cannot be used except when the original package fails or is destroyed.

- Modification to the software is not allowed.

- Decompiling (i.e., reverse engineering) of the program code is not allowed without the permission of the copyright holder.

- Development of new works built upon the package (derivative works) is not allowed without the permission of the copyright holder.

Selling software as *shareware* is a marketing decision; it does not change the legal requirements with respect to copyright. That means that the user can make a single archival copy, but is obliged to pay for all copies adopted for use.

3. Freeware:

Freeware also is covered by copyright and subject to the conditions defined by the holder of the copyright. The conditions for *Freeware* are in direct opposition to normal copyright restrictions. In general, *Freeware* software licenses stipulate that:

- Copies of the software can be made for both archival and distribution purposes but that distribution cannot be for profit.

- Modification of the software is allowed and encouraged.

- Decompiling (i.e., reverse engineering) of the program code is allowed without the explicit permission of the copyright holder; and

- Development of new works built upon the package (derivative works) is allowed and encouraged with the condition that derivative works must also be designated as Freeware.

4. Public Domain:

Public Domain software comes into being when the original copyright holder explicitly relinquishes all rights to the software. Since under current copyright law, all intellectual works (including software) are protected as soon as they are committed to a medium, for something to be *Public Domain* it must be clearly marked as such. Before 1st March 1989, it was assumed that intellectual works were not covered by copyright unless the copyright symbol and declaration appeared on the work. With the U.S. adherence to the Berne Convention this presumption has been reversed. Now all works assume copyright protection unless the Public Domain notification is stated. This means that for *Public Domain* software

- Copyright rights have been relinquished.

- Software copies can be made for both archival and distribution purposes with no restrictions as to distribution.

- Modifications o the software are allowed.

- Decompiling (i.e., reverse engineering) of the program code is allowed; and

- Development of new works built upon the package (derivative works) is allowed without conditions on the distribution or use of the derivative work.

2.3: Trade Mark, Trade Name, Service Marks and Trade Secret

Trademarks:

Trademark is a distinctive sign capable of distinguishing the goods or services produced or provided by one enterprise from those of other enterprises. A trademark may be a "**word, letters, group of letters, numerals, phrase, symbol, design sound, smell, colour, product configuration, logotypes, drawings, pictures, labels or combination of these**, adopted and used by a company to identify and its products or services, and distinguish them from products and services made, sold or provided by other business enterprises. In some countries, **advertising slogans** are also considered trademarks and may be registered as such at national trademark offices.

As increasing number of countries also allow for the registration of less traditional forms of trademarks, such as single colours, three-dimensional signs (shapes of products or packaging), audible signs (sounds) or olfactory signs (smells). However, many countries have set limits on what can be registered as a trademark, generally only allowing for signs that are visually perceptible or that can be represented graphically.

Characteristics of a Trademark:

A trademark is a distinctive sign or indicator of some kind that is used by an individual, business organization or other legal entity to uniquely identify the source of its products and/or services to consumers, and to distinguish its products or services from those of other entities. A trademark is a type of intellectual property.

The owner of a registered trademark may commence legal proceedings for trademark infringement to prevent unauthorized use of that trademark. The trademark is also used informally to refer to any distinguishing attributes by which an individual is readily identified, such as the well known characteristics of celebrities. When trademark is used in relation to services rather than products, it may be called as service marks, particularly in the United States.

A trademark should have the following characteristics:

a) Distinctiveness of the mark means that the mark or get-up is distinct in itself from everything else and no one can justifiably claim the right to use it (e.g., a mark in the shape of an invented work like 'Rin'). Most of the trademarks acquire distinctiveness through use.

b) The trademark should preferably be an invented work.

c) The trademark, if a word or name, should be easy to pronounce and remember, (e.g., 'Bata' for shoes, 'Zen' for car, 'SONY' for electronics; etc.).

d) It must be easy to spell correctly and write legibly.

e) It should not be descriptive but may be suggestive of the quality of goods or services.

f) It should be short.

g) It should have visual as well as audible appeal to the customers.

h) It should satisfy the requirements of registration.

i) It should not belong to the class of marks prohibited for registration.

Functions of Trademark:

The main function of a trademark is to enable consumers to identify a product (whether a good or a service) of a particular company so as similar products provided by competitors and avoid the confusion about the source or origin of a product or service. Marks help the consumers answer the questions – who makes this product? and who provides this service?

A trademark serves the purpose of identifying the source or origin of goods and services. Trademark performs the following functions:

a) It identifies the product and its origin.

b) It guarantees its quality.

c) It advertises the product. Act as a marketing tool and the basis for building a brand image and reputation.

d) It creates an image of the product in the minds of the public, particularly consumers, or the prospective consumers of such goods.

e) Ensures that consumers can distinguish between products.

f) Enable the companies to differentiate their products.

g) Acts as a valuable business asset for the company.

h) Encourage the companies to invest in maintaining or improving product quality, etc.

By enabling companies to **differentiate** themselves and their products from those of the competitors', trademark play a pivotal role in the **branding** and **marketing strategies** of companies, contributing to the definition of the **image** and **reputation** of the company's products in the eyes of consumers. The image and reputation of a company create **trust** which is the basis for establishing a **loyal clientele** and enhancing a **company's goodwill**. Consumers often develop an **emotional attachment** to certain trademarks, based on a set of desired qualities or features embodied in the products bearing such trademarks.

A carefully selected and nurtured trademark is a **valuable business asset** for most of the companies and a registered trademark, as per the trademark law, gives a company the **exclusive right to prevent others** from marketing identical or similar products under the same or confusing similar marks. In addition, it is much easier **to license a registered trademark to other companies**, thus providing an additional source or revenue for the company, or may be the basis for a **franchising agreement**. On various occasions, a registered trademark with a good reputation among consumers may also be used to **obtain funding (mobilize finance)** from the financial institutions that are increasingly aware of the importance of brands for business success.

Guidelines for Registration of Trademark:

Trademark protection can be obtained through **registration** or in some countries also through **use**. Even where the trademarks can be protected through use, it is safe to register the trademark by filing the appropriate application form at the national trademark office (some trademark offices have online registration forms). Registering a trademark will provide stronger protection, particularly in case of conflict with an identical or confusing similar trademark. The services of a trademark agent are often very useful (and sometimes compulsory) for the registration of a trademark.

The questions to be answered – what should be kept in mind when selecting or creating a trademark? and what are the guidelines for registration of trademark?

The Five Point **Checklist** for Selecting a Trademark is:

- Check that the trademark of choice meets all the **legal requirements** for registration.

- Do a **trademark search** to make sure that it is not identical or confusingly similar to existing trademarks.

- Make sure that the trademark is **easy to read, write, spell** and **remember** and is suitable to all types of advertising media.

- Make sure that the mark does not have **undesired connotations** in any language of potential export markets.

- Check the corresponding **domain name** (i.e., internet address) is available for registration.

The major **guidelines** to be followed are:

a) Trademark application can be filed for a mark which is in 'USE' or 'PROPOSED TO BE USED.' It is considered as an inseparable part of the goodwill of the business and is being considered as '**Movable Property.**'

b) The Proprietor or Director or Managing Partner should authorize your attorney or agent under **Form TM-48** to appear before the Registrar on behalf of the firm/company. It would be on non-judicial stamp paper. If the firm authorize in Form TM- 48, the attorney or agent is entitled to sign in all papers to be filed for registration except affidavit. The firm has to furnish the **First Date** from which the mark is being continuously used. The can be verified from the firm's first sales invoice.

c) Furnish the name of the proprietor or name of all partners in the firm and address of the firm or company. If it is a private/public limited company, please furnish the **Memorandum** and **Articles of Association.**

d) The firm/company has to furnish **20 labels** of its mark, if such mark contains any lettering style or logo or device or label, it should be in small size. Otherwise, furnish the 'word' itself. Labels should be mounted upon the **Form TM-1** in triplicate and on ten additional representations.

e) Furnish the specification of goods to which the mark is applicable.

f) After filing, computerized application number will be allotted to the firm's mark within **FORTY** days from the date of filing application. Then the firm has to pass the following three stages during the period of four to five years or to some extent.

- Examination stage

- Enquiry stage by Registrar

- Advertisement Stage – TRADEMARKS JOURNAL

- Opposition stage, if any.

g) While the firm's case is pending, the firm can use the trademark as it wishes. 'User' is very important in trademarks. The firm/company will gain goodwill because of the continuous use of the mark. For better protection, the firm/company has to get registration of the trademark.

While selecting one or more words as trademark the firm/company should also take into consideration the implication of selecting certain **types of words**:

- A **Coined or 'fanciful' (inherently distinctive) words** – these are invented words without any intrinsic or real meaning (e.g., Kodak).

- **Arbitrary marks** – these are words that have meaning that has no relation to the product they advertise (e.g., "Apple" for computers).

- **Suggestive marks** – these are marks that hint at one or some of the attributes of the product or service. The appeal of suggestive marks is that they act as a form of advertising. The suggestive marks indicate the nature, quality or the characteristics of the product or services. Suggestive marks invoke the consumer's perceptive imagination. (e.g., the trademark SUNNY for marketing electric heaters would hint at the fact that the product is meant to radiate heat and keep things warm. Moreover, EASY WEAR is a registered trademark for teenage clothing)

Once the trademark is registered, the life of the trademark is generally valid for 10 years and renewable indefinitely by paying the required renewal fees, but the registration may be canceled entirely for certain good or services if the trademark has not been used for a certain period of time specified in the relevant trademark law.

Signs Excluded from Registration (Marks Not Registrable):

What are the main reasons for rejecting an application for the registration of trademark?

While selecting a trademark, it is helpful to know which categories of signs (marks) are usually not acceptable for registration. Most jurisdictions totally exclude certain types of terms and symbols from registration as trademarks, including the emblems, insignia and flags of nations, certain organizations and the modern Olympic Games, marks which are deceptive as to the origin of their associated products or services, and marks comprising signs that are contrary to accepted principles of morality (e.g., the marks which obscene). Applications for trademark registration are usually rejected on what are commonly referred to as "**absolute grounds**" in the following cases:

- Generic Terms – if the company intents, for example, to register the trademark CHAIR to sell chairs, the mark would be rejected since "chair" is the generic term for the product.

- Descriptive Terms – these are words that are usually used in trade to describe the product in question. For example, the use of the word SWEET for the products likes chocolates.

- Deceptive Trademarks – these are the trademarks that are likely to deceive or mislead consumers as to the nature, quality or geographical origin of the product.

- Contrary to Public Order or Morality – the marks considered being contrary to the commonly accepted norms of public order or morality and religion are normally not allowed to be registered as trademarks.

- Flags, armorial bearings, official hallmarks and emblems of states and international organizations – which have been communicated to the International Bureau of WIPO, are usually excluded from registration.

- A word which is the accepted name of any single chemical name or chemical compound in respect of chemical substances.

- A geographical name, a surname, a personal name, any common abbreviation thereof or the name of a sect, caste, tribe, etc.

Applications are rejected on "**relative grounds**" when the trademark conflicts with **prior trademark rights**. Having two identical or very similar trademarks for the same type of product could cause confusion among consumers. It would, therefore, be wise to avoid using trademarks that risk being considered confusingly conflicting with similar existing marks.

Non-Traditional Trademarks:

There are many less familiar types of trademarks, which may be described as non-traditional trademarks. Some of the types of the less traditional (non-traditional) trademarks are:

a) **Appearance** – This type of mark may include the colour or combination of colours applied to the products themselves or to the packaging in which they are sold. It may be the graphical way in which the colours are represented or a combination of both. In the case of services, it could include the visual appearance, externally or internally, of a store or restaurant or the design of a menu card.

b) **Shape** – This type of the mark may be a three – dimensional representation of the product itself, the container for the product, the architectural design of a store or sign-post. It may be the shape of a label or tag and not simply the words or colours appearing thereon.

c) **Sounds** – This type of mark may be a jingle or any piece of music or other sound. It may be a short extract from a composition or an entire musical piece. In some cases, it may be a reproduction of an everyday sound, perhaps in an unusual circumstance.

d) **Scents (Smell)** – In terms of registration of trademarks, this type of mark is one of the most difficult to represent graphically. Many smells are associated, however, with a particular manufacturer. In some cases, such a perfume houses, the particular scent is also the product itself. In other cases, it is a scent applied or added to the product, not the natural smell of the product itself.

e) **Taste** – In many cases it will be difficult to distinguish between the natural flavour of a product and the recipe adopted by a manufacturer to distinguish its goods from those of the competitors.' The flavour of Coca Cola is a good example. The manufacturer of such goods would certainly consider the flavour of their products as being a trademark of the company and the recipes are often closely-guarded trade secrets.

f) **Touch** – It is possible for product to be manufactured in such a way that the products or their packaging have a particular sensation to the touch, which can distinguish them from those competitors. Sometimes, a particular feel will reflect the quality of the product rather tan the origin, but this type of mark may include, for example, tissues that are particularly soft or moist or products that may be held in the hand more comfortably. It is common practice for some products to have writing in Braille applied to them. Similarly registrable features may be added to products.

Major Types of Trademarks:

The trademarks broadly classified into following major types:

1.	Trade marks:	Marks used to distinguish certain goods as those produced by a specific enterprise.
2.	Service marks:	Marks used to distinguish certain services as those provided by a specific enterprise. Services may be of any kind, such as financial, banking, travel, advertising, catering, and so on. Service marks can be registered, renewed, assigned and licensed under the same conditions as trademarks.

3. Certification marks: Marks used to distinguish goods and services that comply with a set of standards and have been certified by a certifying authority. The Certification marks are given for compliance with defined standards, but are not confined to any membership. They may be used by anyone whose products meet certain established standards. In many countries, the main difference between collective marks and certification marks is that the former may only be used by a specific group of enterprises, e.g., members of an association, while certification marks may be used by anybody who complies with standards defined by the owner of the certification mark. An important requirement for certification marks is that the entity which applies for registration is considered "competent to certify" the products concerned.

4. Well – known marks: Marks that are considered to be well-known in the market and as a result benefit from stronger protection. These are the marks may be protected even if not registered (or have not been used) in a given territory.

5. Collective marks: Marks used to distinguish goods or services produced or provided by members of an association. A collective mark is generally owned by an association or cooperative whose members may use the collective mark to market their products. The association generally established a set of criteria for using the collective mark (e.g., quality standards) and permits individual companies to use the mark if they comply with such standards. Collective marks may be an effective way of jointly marketing the product of a group of enterprises which may find it more difficult for their individual marks to be recognized by consumers and/or handled by the main distributors.

2.4: Industrial Design

Industrial Design generally refers to a product's overall form and function. From an intellectual property law perspective, an industrial design refers only to the ornamental or aesthetic aspects of a product. Although the design of a product may have technical aor functional features, industrial design, as a category of intellectual property law, refers only to the aesthetic nature of a finished product, and is distinct from an technical or functional aspects.

Industrial design is relevant to a wide variety of products of industry, fashion and handicrafts from technical and medical instruments to watches, jewelry, and other luxury items; from household products, toys, furniture and electrical appliances to cars and architectural structures; from textile design to sports equipment. Industrial design is also important in relation to packaging, containers and "get-up" of products.

As a general rule, an industrial design consists of:

- Three-dimensional features, such as the shape of a product.

- Two-dimensional features, such as ornamentation, patterns, lines or colour of a product.

- A combination of one or more of such features.

Importance (Need) of Industrial Design:

The business enterprises often devote a significant amount of time and resources to enhancing the design appeal of their products. New and original designs often created to:

1. **Customize products to appeal to specific market segments** – small modification to the design of some products may make them suitable for different age groups, cultures or social groups.

2. **Create a new niche market** – in a competitive marketplace, many companies seek to create a niche market by introducing creative designs for their new products to differentiate them from those of their competitors. This could be the case for ordinary items such as locks, shoes, cups and saucers to potentially expensive items such as jewelry, computers, cars, etc.

3. **Strengthen brands** – creative designs are often also combined with distinctive trademarks to enhance the distinctiveness of a company's brand(s). Many companies have successfully created or redefined their brand image through a strong focus on product design.

4. **Adds value to the product** – it makes a product attractive and appealing to customers and may even be its unique selling point.

5. **Obtain exclusive right** – to prevent unauthorized copying or imitation by others.

6. **Source of additional revenue** – i.e., the protected design may also be licensed or sold to others for a fee or price.

7. Strengthen the competitive power and to earn a fair return on investment.

8. Promote and encourage creativity – it increases interest in innovating more designs in the field of consumer products.

Essential Requirements for the Registration of Design:

- What can be registered as an Industrial Design?

As a general rule, essential requirements to be registered, a design must meet one or more of the following, depending on the law of the country.

- The design must be "**new**." A design is considered to be new if no identical design has been made available to the public before the date of filing, or the application for registration.

- The design must be "**original**." A design is considered original if it has been independently created by the designer and is not a copy or an imitation of existing designs.

- The design must have "**individual character**." This requirement is met if the overall impression produced by a design on an informed user differs from the overall impression produced on such a user by any earlier design which has been made available to the public.

- The design should relate to features of shape, configuration, pattern or ornamentation applied or applicable to an article.

- The design should be applied or applicable to any article by any industrial process.

- The features of the design in the finished article should appeal to and are judged solely by the eye. This implies that the design must appear and should be visible on the finished article, for which it is meant.

- The design should not include any trademark or property mark.

- It should be significantly distinguishable from known designs or combination of known designs.

- It should not comprise or contain scandalous or obscene matter.

In the **digital world**, design protection is gradually extending in some countries to a number of other products and types of design. These include electronic desktop icons generated by computer codes, typefaces, the graphic display on computer monitors and mobile telephones, etc.

Exclusion from the scope of Design Protection:

- What cannot be protected by industrial design rights?

Designs that are generally barred from registration in many countries include the following:

- Designs that do not meet the requirements of **novelty, originality** and **individual character.**

- Designs that considered to be dictated exclusively by the **technical function** of a product.

- Designs incorporating protected **official symbols** or **emblems**.

- Designs which are considered to be **contrary to public order or morality**.

- Designs that are primarily literary or artistic in character are not protected under the Designs Act, and will include:

  ➢ Book jackets, calendars, certificates, forms and other documents, dressmaking patterns, greeting cards, leaflets, maps and plans cards, post cards, stamps, transfers, medals

  ➢ Labels, tokens, cartoons

  ➢ Any principle or mode of construction of an article

  ➢ Mere mechanical contrivance

  ➢ Buildings and structures

  ➢ Parts of articles not manufactured and sold separately

  ➢ Variations commonly used in the trade

  ➢ Mere workshop alterations of components of an assembly

  ➢ Mere change in the size of article

  ➢ Lay-out designs of integrated circuits, etc.

In addition, it is important to note that some countries exclude **handicrafts** from design protection, as industrial design law in these countries requires that the product to which an industrial design is applied is "an article of manufacture" or that it can be replicated by "industrial means."

Depending on the national legislation there may be further restrictions on what cannot be registered as a design. It is advisable to consult an IP agent or the relevant national IP office for an authentic understanding of what can and what cannot be registered under design rights.

Grace Period and Duration (Tenure/Term) of Design Patent:

In some countries, the legislation allows for a grace period for registration of generally six months or a year from the moment a design was made public, disclosed or published.

This is the case when articles bearing the design are sold, displayed at a trade show, exhibition or fair, or are published in a catalogue, brochure or advertisement prior to filing an application. During that period, one can market his or her design without it losing its "novelty" and he or she can still apply for registration.

However, as this is not the case in all countries, and, in any event, is limited in time, it is often advisable to keep the design confidential until one applies for design protection. In addition, he or she will have no exclusive design rights during the grace period (although the design may be automatically protected under copyright or unfair competition law, depending on the provisions of the relevant national legislation).

How long does industrial design protection last?

The term of protection for a registered industrial design varies from country to country, but is usually at least 10 years (although it is often longer, for example, 14 years for design patent in the United States of America, and up to 25 years under the registered Community Design of the European Union). In many countries, rights holders are required to renew their design protection after five years. Moreover, most countries require the payment of renewal fees, usually on a five year basis, to maintain their exclusive rights over an industrial design.

Protecting Designs Abroad:

If the company intends to export products bearing an original design, or intends to license the manufacture, sale or export of such products to other firms in foreign countries, it should consider protecting its design in such countries in order to enjoy the same benefits of protection abroad as it enjoys in the domestic market.

How to Protect Industrial Design abroad?

Industrial design protection is territorial. This means that industrial design is generally limited to the country or region where it has been registered. Hence, if one wishes to have his or her industrial design protected in export markets, it essential to make sure that protection is applied for in those specific countries.

It is important to bear in mind that one will usually have six months from the date on which applied for protection in the first country to claim the right of priority while applying for design protection in other countries. Once this period has lapsed, it is not possible to apply for design protection in foreign countries, as the design will no longer be considered new.

There are three ways of protecting the industrial designs abroad:

1. The National Route: Companies may seek protection by applying separately to the national IP offices of each country in which they intend to obtain protection. The process can be rather cumbersome and expensive as translation into the national languages is generally required as well as payment of administrative (and sometimes legal) fees.

2. The Regional Route: If you are interested in a group of countries that are members of regional agreements which enable the registration of designs in more than one country, then you can consider filing a single application at the regional IP office concerned. Regional IP offices include:

- *The African Regional Industrial Property Office (ARIPO) for industrial design protection in English speaking African countries.*

- *The BENELUX Designs Office (BDO) for protection in Belgium, the Netherlands and Luxembourg.*

- *The Office for Harmonization in the Internal Market (OHIM) for Community designs in the countries of the European Union.*

- *The Organization Africaine de la Propriete Intellectuelle (OAPI) for protection in French speaking African countries.*

3. The International Route: Companies that wish to register their designs internationally in several countries may also use the procedures offered by the ***Hague Agreement Concerning the International Deposit of Industrial Designs***, a WIPO – administered treaty. An applicant from a Member Country to the Hague Agreement can file a single international application with WIPO; the design will then be protected in as many Member Countries of the treaty as the applicant wishes. The agreement provides applicants with a simpler and cheaper mechanism for applying for industrial design registration in various countries.

The **costs** of an industrial design registration under the Hague Agreement vary depending on the number of designs to be protected and the number of countries where protection is sought. For example, the cost of protection for five designs in 11 countries using the international route offered by the Hague system is approximately 900 Swiss francs.

2.5: Layout Designs of Integrated Circuits

A layout-design of an integrated circuit is the three-dimensional disposition of the elements of an integrated circuit and some or all of the interconnections of the integrated circuit or such three-dimensional disposition prepared for an integrated circuit intended for manufacture.

Integrated circuits (often called "chips") are the core components of the information technology industry. They are essential components in any digital equipment, and have been incorporated into a great variety of other industrial articles, ranging from machine tools to all kinds of household and consumer devices. Integrated circuits consist of an electronic circuitry developed on the basis of a tri-dimensional design,incorporated into a substrate, generally a solid sheet of semiconductor material,typically silicon, and less commonly germanium or gallium arsenide. Integrated circuits comprise a range of products (microprocessors, dynamic memories, programmable logic devices, etc.). Both the design and, particularly, the production of such circuits require, because of the microscopic size of the transistors and other electronic components inserted into a chip, significant technical capabilities and heavy investments in plant facilities. The manufacturing technologies and production plants are under the control of a relatively small number of companies mainly from the USA and Japan. South Korea, Taiwan Province of China and Singapore have actively supported the development of a local semiconductor industry, while China, Ireland, Israel, Malaysia and, more recently, Costa Rica, have pursued investments of foreign semiconductor manufacturers(Chap.27 CY564-Unctad-v1 November 29, 2004)

The layout-designs of integrated circuits are creations of human mind. It takes enormous investment, both in terms of time and money, to design a new layout-design. But a chip pirate can easily replicate the layout-design of a chip in few months by removing the chips plastic/ceramic casing and photographing each layer of the translucent silicon material; at a fraction of the original cost (Senate Report No 425, 98th Cong, 2d Session 8 (1984)). Before 2003, the legal framework relating to copyright, patent or industrial designs did not afford adequate protection to layout-designs. Firstly, protection of layout-designs demands more stringent norms of originality than those required under the Copyright Act. The Copyright Act is too general to accommodate the original ideas of scientific creation of layout-designs. Also whilst it may well have been the case that any design drawings and the masks used in the production process would benefit from copyright protection, the status of the finished product was less clear. Just as copyright in an architectural plan does not prevent anyone from building the house represented in that plan 4, copyright in the technical drawings representing a chip design does not protect against unauthorized duplication of the chip itself. Secondly, for an article to receive a patent, its design must be novel and non-obvious. This high standard of inventiveness required of patentable articles is rarely achieved in what is essentially the spatial organization of commonly known circuit elements. Thus the work involved in chip manufacturing is of a developmental nature rather than an inventive nature and might not qualify for a patent(Patents (Amendment) Act, 2005,) . Thirdly, layout-designs of integrated circuits are not industrial designs because they do not determine the external appearance of integrated circuits. They determine the physical location, within the integrated circuit, of each element having an electronic function. Thus, the need was felt for *sui generis* protection.

The Semiconductor Integrated Circuits Layout-Design Act, 2000 (the 'Act') gives recognition to a new form of intellectual property, namely, the 'layout-designs' used in semiconductor integrated circuits (TRIPS agreement) as has been defined u/s 2(h) of the Act. Exchange of information on a worldwide basis now can occur instantaneously because it can be stored so readily and in such quantities in semiconductor integrated circuits or chips as they are commonly known, has far reaching implications for privacy, international relations, national security and defense. Chips are often referred to as 'the crude oil of the information age'(A J W Van de Gevel, 2000).

The simplest integrated circuit consists of three layers, one of which is made from semiconductor material. A wafer (i.e. a thin, highly polished silicon crystal disk) of semiconductor material is coated with a layer of silicon oxide (an insulator) and the electronic components (for example, transistors) are formed by a process of diffusion (chemically doping the semiconductor material with impurities through holes etched through the oxide). Finally, an aluminium coating is applied which is partly evaporated using a mask, leaving behind the interconnections between components formed in the semiconductor layer. It might thus be said that that the information highway is paved with silicon. The mask is transparent except for opaque patterns on the mask that correspond to the circuit patterns to be etched into the wafer. In a complex circuit, another layer of silicon is placed on top of the etched wafer, and the same etching process is repeated. A chip typically has eight to twelve layers, each layer having a unique mask creating the required circuits. These layers of masks, collectively called 'mask work' or 'layout-design', manifest the three-dimensional layout of the chip. It is a chip's layout, or three-dimensional organization that requires protection. In more advanced manufacturing systems, the actual physical mask may be dispensed with and the semiconductor material may be subjected to a controlled light beam which effectively traces out (in raster fashion) a mask for each layer of the chip. Hereafter, references to 'masks' should be read as including the stored information used in controlled light beam, as well as the more conventional photographic type physical 'mask.'(Atul Gupta, JIPR, 2005)

Protection of Integrated Circuits Layout-Design

The Washington Treaty of 1989, which came about as the result of international efforts to harmonize the law relating to the protection of semiconductor integrated circuit layout designs, defines an integrated circuit as:

[A] product, in its final form or an intermediate form, in which the elements, at least one of which is an active element, and some or all of the interconnections are integrally formed in and/or on a piece of material and which is intended to perform an electronic function.

'Layout design' is defined as . . . the three-dimensional disposition, however expressed, of the elements, at least one of which is an active element, and of some or all of the interconnections of an integrated circuit, or such a three-dimensional disposition prepared for an integrated circuit intended for manufacture. 24 In addition to giving the scope of protection, the Washington Treaty provides a defence of reverse engineering under Article 6(2), which states: (2) [Acts Not Requiring the Authorization of the Holder of the Right]

a) Notwithstanding paragraph (1), no Contracting Party shall consider unlawful the performance,without the authorization of the holder of the right,of the act of reproduction referred to in paragraph (1)(a)(i) where that act is performed by a third party for private purposes or for the sole purpose of evaluation, analysis, research or teaching.

b) Where the third party referred to in subparagraph (a), on the basis of evaluation or analysis of the pro- tected layout-design (topography) ('the first layout- design (topography)'), creates a layout-design (topography) complying with the requirement of originality referred to in Article 3(2) ('the second layout- design (topography)'), that third party may incorporate the second layout-design (topography) in an integrated circuit or perform any of the acts referred to in paragraph (1) in respect of the second layout-design (topography) without being regarded as infringing the rights of the holder of the right in the first layout-design (topography).

c) The holder of the right may not exercise his right in respect of an identical original layout-design (topography) that was independently created by a third party.

This provision of the Washington Treaty can be recognized in Article 35 of TRIPS, which applies some of the provisions of the Washington Treaty mutatis mutandis.(Saurabh Bindal, JIPLP, 2015)

2.6: Geographical Indication (GI)

Most of us know of many products that represent a GI and yet may not be aware of their ubiquitousness. They range from Champagne, Scotch whisky, and Port ine to Idaho potatoes, Roquefort cheese, and Kona coffee. All are registered Geographical Indications (GIs), sometimes called appellations, that represent a very successful form of differentiation and competitive advantage in today's markets. GIs are a unique expression of local agro-ecological and cultural characteristics that have come to be valued and protected in many countries throughout the world. Besides the well-known GIs from more developed regions, there are also a number from developing regions such as Darjeeling tea, Aranyik knives, Basmati rice, and Pisco liquor. However, not all GIs are popular or successful.

In India Article 22 contains the basic definition of 'geographical indication' applicable toall protect and describes the general level of protection available in respect of the same.

There is no universally accepted definition of a GI, but this description, derived from international agreements best captures the universal spirit of the concept:

A Geographical Indication identifies a good as originating in a delimited territory or region where a noted quality, reputation or other characteristic of the good is essentially attributable to its geographical origin and/or the human or natural factors there. In most cases, GIs have been formally used and accepted as such in trade and in legal records. They may be registered or protected in different forms; these can include formal *sui generis* systems, trademarks, certification marks, collective membership marks, and denominations of origin. Sometimes, they are not formally protected and may be recognized due to accepted common use. In many cases, certain GIs are protected in one country but not in another or the forms and scope of protection are often different from country to country. For example Feta and Champagne are protected in the European Union but not in the United States where the words can be used generically.

A GI is a unique and important form of collective intellectual and cultural property, with various rights. The right to the exclusive use of a name, which typically defines a specific geographic (or sometimes cultural) area, is given by the State to regional producers and processors of particular products for their use only in relation to those products. It is expected that there is a direct link between the distinguishing characteristics, cultural aspects or the quality of a product and the place of origin or geographic area. Hence, the GI is a device that signals a set of unique qualities or attributes to consumers. The term "Geographical Indication" has been around for many decades, but it is really since the WTO Agreement on Trade-Related Aspects of Intellectual Property Rights (TRIPS) entered into force in the mid-1990s, that it has come into common use. The TRIPS Agreement, Article 22, paragraph 1 contains the following description: Geographical indications are, for the purposes of this Agreement, indications which identify a good as originating in the territory of a Member, or a region or locality in that territory, where a given quality, reputation or other characteristic of the good is essentially attributable to its geographic origin.

GIs became popular because they perceived to offer a wide range of opportunities that go beyond the economic and beyond the interests of their producers at origin. Like trade standards, GIs provide certain information and offer a guarantee. From a consumer's point of view, GIs signal important characteristics that may not be obvious or evident by simply inspecting the product. For example, consumers cannot easily determine the qualities of a wine, or its production process, or whether a cheese is made according to a traditional method. 6 A GI confirms a link not only between a product and a specific geographic region, but usually also with unique production methods, characteristics or qualities that are known to exist in the region.(Guide to Geographical Indications: Linking products and their origins, Geneva ITC, 2009)

Registration of GI in India [Ahuja V.K, 2004]

➢ Section 11(2) of the GI Act specifies the documentation requirements for applying for a GI in India. Section 32(1) of the GI Rules replicates these provisions and in addition stipulates a few more documentation requirements that include the following:

➢ A statement as to how the GI serves to designate the goods as originating from the concerned geographical territory in respect of specific quality, reputation or other characteristics that are due exclusively or essentially to the geographical environment, with its inherent natural and human factors; and the production, processing or preparation of which takes place in such geographical location.

➢ The geographical map of the territory concerned.

➢ The particulars regarding the appearance of the GI as to whether it is comprised of the words or figurative elements or both.

➢ An affidavit as to how the applicant claims to represent the interest of the association of persons or producers or any organization or authority established by or under any law

➢ The standards benchmark for the use of the GI or the industry standard as regards the production, exploitation, making or manufacture of the goods having specific quality, reputation, or other characteristic of such goods that is essentially attributable to its geographical origin with the detailed description of the human creativity involved, if any, or other characteristic from the definite geographical territory.

➢ The particulars of the mechanism to ensure that the standards, quality, integrity and consistency or other special characteristic in respect of the goods to which the GI relates, which are maintained by the producers, makers or manufacturers of the goods, as the case may be.

> ➤ The particulars of special human skill involved or the uniqueness of the geographical environment or other inherent characteristics associated with the GI to which the application relates.

> ➤ The particulars of the inspection structure, if any, to regulate the use of the GI in respect of the goods for which application is made in the definite territory, region or locality mentioned in the application

2.7: Emerging Forms-Traditional Knowledge and Domain Name

Traditional Knowledge (TK)

Human communities have always generated, refined and passed on knowledge from generation to generation. Such "traditional" knowledge" is often an important part of their cultural identities. Traditional knowledge has played, and still plays, a vital role in the daily lives of the vast majority of people. Traditional knowledge is essential to the food security and health of millions of people in the developing world. In many countries, traditional medicines provide the only affordable treatment available to poor people. In developing countries, up to 80% of the population depend on traditional medicines to help meet their healthcare needs. In addition, knowledge of the healing properties of plants has been the source of many modern medicines. As it is noted the use and continuous development by local farmers of plant varieties and the sharing and diffusion of these varieties and the knowledge associated with them play an essential role in agricultural systems in developing countries.

Only recently, however, has the international community sought to recognise and protect traditional knowledge. In 1981, WIPO and UNESCO adopted a model law on folklore. In 1989 the concept of Farmers' Rights was introduced by the FAO into its International Undertaking on Plant Genetic Resources and in 1992 the Convention on Biological Diversity (CBD) highlighted the need to promote and preserve traditional knowledge. In spite of these efforts which have spanned two decades, final and universally acceptable solutions for the protection and promotion of traditional knowledge have not yet emerged.

The CBD also set out principles governing access to genetic resources and the knowledge associated with them, and the sharing of benefits arising from such access. We therefore consider the relationship between the IP system and the access and benefit sharing principles of the CBD in the context of both knowledge, traditional or otherwise, and genetic resources.

Background of TK

A number of cases relating to traditional knowledge have attracted international attention. As a result, the issue of traditional knowledge has been brought to the fore of the general debate surrounding intellectual property. These cases involve what is often referred to as "biopiracy" (See Chapter 5). The examples of turmeric and neem illustrate the issues that can arise when patent protection is granted to inventions relating to traditional knowledge which is already in the public domain. In these cases, invalid patents were issued because the patent examiners were not aware of the relevant traditional knowledge. In another example, a patent was granted on a plant species called Hoodia. Here, the issue was not whether the patent should or should not have been granted, but rather on whether the local people known as the San, who had nurtured the traditional knowledge underpinning the invention, were entitled to receive a fair share of any benefits arising from commercialization.

Partly as a result of these well known cases, many developing countries, holders of traditional knowledge, and campaigning organizations are pressing in a multitude of fora for traditional knowledge to be better protected. Such pressure has led, for example, to the creation of an Intergovernmental Committee on

Intellectual Property and Genetic Resources, Traditional Knowledge and Folklore in WIPO. The protection of traditional knowledge and folklore is also being discussed within the framework of the CBD and in other international organizations such as UNCTAD, WHO, FAO and UNESCO. 6 In addition, the Doha WTO Ministerial Declaration highlighted the need for further work in the TRIPS Council on protecting traditional knowledge.

How to define Traditional knowledge with IPR prospective?

There is no widely acceptable definition for Traditional knowledge. It is not only the broad scope of traditional knowledge that has confounded the debate so far. There is also some confusion about exactly what is meant by "protection" and its purpose. It should certainly not be equated directly with the use of the word "protection" in its IP sense. In its report on a series of fact-finding missions, WIPO sought to summarize the concerns of traditional knowledge holders as follows:

- concern about the loss of traditional life styles and of traditional knowledge, and the reluctance of the younger members of the communities to carry forward traditional practices.

- Concern about the lack of respect for traditional knowledge and holders of traditional knowledge.

- Concern about the misappropriation of traditional knowledge including use of traditional knowledge without any benefit sharing, or use in a derogatory manner

- Lack of recognition of the need to preserve and promote the further use of traditional knowledge.

A 2002 World Intellectual Property Organization (WIPO) report on the intellectual property needs and expectations of traditional knowledge holders includes in the traditional knowledge sub-category:

"tradition-based literary, artistic and scientific works, performances, inventions, scientific discoveries, designs, marks, names and symbols, undisclosed information and all other tradition-based innovations and creations resulting from intellectual activity in the industrial, scientific, literary or artistic field."

Further, according to WIPO:

"Contrary to a common perception, traditional knowledge is not necessarily ancient. It is evolving all the time, a process of periodic, even daily creation as individuals and communities take up the challenges presented by their social and physical environment. In many ways therefore, traditional knowledge is actually contemporary knowledge. Traditional knowledge is embedded in traditional knowledge systems, which each community has developed and maintained in its local context. The commercial and other advantages deriving from that use could give rise to intellectual property questions that could in turn be multiplied by international trade, communications and cultural exchange. (Djims Milius, Thomson Reuters (Legal) Ltd. and Contributors,2009)

How to protect Traditional knowledge?

Examples are emerging which illustrate how the current intellectual property system can be utilised to commercialise traditional knowledge or prevent its misuse. For example, Aboriginal and Torres Strait Islander artists in Australia have obtained a national certification trademark. Like any other trademark, this certification mark or Label of Authenticity is intended to help promote the marketing of their art and cultural products and deter the sale of products falsely claiming to be of Aboriginal origin.

In recent surveys of the existing protection of traditional knowledge and folklore, a number of countries have provided further examples of how IP tools have been utilized to promote and protect traditional knowledge and folklore. These include the use of copyright protection in Canada to protect tradition-based creations including masks, totem poles and sound recordings of Aboriginal artists; the use of industrial designs to protect the external appearance of articles such as head dresses and carpets in Kazakhstan and the use of geographical indications to protect traditional products such as liquors, sauces and teas in Venezuela and Vietnam.

The ability to extend the life of trademarks indefinitely and the possibility of collective ownership of such rights suggest that they may be especially suitable for protecting traditional knowledge. This is also the case with geographical indications, which may be used to protect traditional products or crafts if particular characteristics of such products can be attributed to a particular geographical origin. However, trademarks and geographical indications can only prevent the use of the protected marks or indications; they do not protect the knowledge, or the technologies embracing that knowledge, as such.

Other IP rights, especially those requiring some form of novelty or those with fairly limited periods of protection, seem less appropriate for protecting traditional knowledge. Nevertheless it is clear from these surveys, and indeed other research, that existing IPRs do have a role to play in protecting traditional knowledge. Whether that role is a significant one remains to be seen. Experience elsewhere would suggest that the impact may not be great, not least because of the high cost of obtaining and enforcing rights. If the majority of small companies in developed countries have found the intellectual property system, particularly the patent system, to be unattractive, then it seems unlikely that local communities in developing countries, or individuals within such communities, will derive much benefit.

Some countries have already decided that the existing intellectual property system is not, on its own, adequate to protect traditional knowledge. A number of these have enacted or are in the process of enacting *sui generis* systems of protection.

The Philippines has enacted legislation, and is considering further provisions, giving indigenous communities rights over their traditional knowledge. These rights extend to controlling access to ancestral lands, access to biological and genetic resources and to indigenous knowledge related to these resources. Access by other parties will be based on the prior informed consent (PIC) of the community obtained in accordance with customary laws. Any benefits arising from genetic resources or associated knowledge will be equitably shared. The legislation however seeks to maintain the free exchange of biodiversity among local communities. The law also seeks to ensure that indigenous communities are able to participate at all levels of decision-making.

According to WIPO practical guide on 'Intellectual Property and Folk, Arts and Cultural Festivals'

To this day, Traditional knowledge (TK) and Traditional Cultural Expressions (TCEs), unless secret or protected through some special legislation, are generally regarded by conventional IP systems as being in the public domain. However, indigenous peoples and others question this. At the international level, unlike most conventional forms of IP, TK and TCEs are not directly protected through IP law, save for the protection of performances of expressions of folklore under the WIPO Performances and Phonograms Treaty, 1996, and the Beijing Treaty on Audiovisual Performances, 2012.

This does not mean that TK and TCEs can be used freely at any festival. Works that are based on TCEs may be protected by copyright or related rights: for example, a film of a traditional ceremony will likely be protected as a cinematographic work, recording of a song will attract related rights, a contemporary adaptation of a folksong is probably protected under copyright, and photographs of traditional costumes may not be used without the photographer's permission. In these examples, the use of the work based on the TCE may require prior authorization as is the case for any copyrighted work.

Moreover, the rights of indigenous peoples are addressed in the United Nations Declaration on the Rights of Indigenous Peoples, 2007. Under this Declaration, as well as under some national laws, indigenous people have the right to maintain, control, protect and develop their IP over cultural heritage, TK and TCEs.

Traditional Knowledge Digital Library (TKDL) – An Indian View

In 1999, following the ultimately successful, but expensive, Indian challenge of the turmeric and basmati patents granted by USPTO, it was agreed that the Indian National Institute of Science Communication (NISCOM) and the Department of Indian System of Medicine and Homoeopathy (ISM&H) would collaborate to establish a Traditional Knowledge Digital Library (TKDL).

The TKDL project is initially targeting Ayurveda (a traditional Indian system of medicine), and proposes to document the knowledge available in public domain (the existing Ayurveda literature) in digitised format. Information from about 35,000 Slokas (Versus & Prose) and formulations will be inputted on a database, and it is expected that the web site will have approximately 140,000 Ayurveda pages. The data will be made available in several international languages (English, Spanish, German, French, Japanese and Hindi).

The Traditional Knowledge Resource Classification (TKRC) is an innovative, structured classification system that has been designed to facilitate the systematic arrangement, dissemination and retrieval of the information in the traditional knowledge DL. The TKRC is based on the International Patent Classification system (IPC), with the information classified under section, class, subclass, group and subgroup for the convenience of its use by the international patent examiners. But it provides greater definition of traditional knowledge information by expanding one IPC group (i.e. AK61K35/78 related to medicinal plants) into about 5000 subgroups.

The TKDL will give legitimacy to existing traditional knowledge, and by ensuring ease of retrieval of traditional knowledge-related information by patent examiners will hopefully prevent the granting of patents, such as the turmeric and neem cases discussed above which claim subject matter already in the public domain.

Work on such libraries is also being pursued in WIPO where a specialized Task Force including representatives from China, India, the USPTO, and the EPO are examining how such libraries can be integrated into the existing search tools used by patent offices.

Domain Name

Domain Names are the names for the information's address on the Internet and are used to locate information on the Internet. This has been possible due to Domain Name System (DNS), which translates these domain names to the IP addresses of the computers.

The Internet Corporation for Assigned Names and Numbers (ICANN) is responsible for the administration of Top Level Domain Names.

The domain names are allocated by the administrator of the Top Level Domain (TLD), if the requested domain name is not already assigned previoulsy.

The management and operations of .IN Registry are managed by the National Internet Exchange of India (NIXI). IN Registry is now the official registry for registration but this registry does not carry out the functions itself, but through accredits registrars.

Like a trademark, a domain name too is associated with a particular firm and creates a unique identity. In today's world when most of the work is done on the World Wide Web it can help preventing other people from misleading customers. Hence it is very important to get a domain name registered.

What is a domain name?

Domain names are the human-friendly forms of Internet addresses, and are commonly used to find web sites. For example, the domain name wipo.int is used to locate the WIPO web site at http://www.wipo.int or the WIPO Arbitration and Mediation Center site at http://www.wipo.int/amc/. A domain name also forms the basis of other methods or applications on the Internet, such as file transfer (ftp) or email addresses - for example the email address arbiter.mail@wipo.int is also based on the domain name wipo.int.

What is the domain name system (DNS)?

The domain name system is essentially a global addressing system. It is the way that domain names are located and translated into Internet Protocol (IP) addresses, and vice versa. A domain name such as wipo. int is a unique alias for an IP address (a number), which is an actual physical point on the Internet.

What is a gTLD?

A gTLD is a generic top level domain. It is the top-level domain of an Internet address, for example: .com, .net and .org. In addition, seven new gTLDs were also selected by ICANN (the Internet Corporation for Assigned Names and Numbers) on November 16, 2000. These are: .aero (for the entire aviation community); .biz (for business purposes); .coop (for cooperatives); .info (unrestricted); .museum (for museums); .name (for personal names); .pro (for professionals).

What is a ccTLD?

A ccTLD is a country code top-level domain, for example: .mx for Mexico. These ccTLDs are administered independently by nationally designated registration authorities. There are currently 252 ccTLDs reflected in the database of the Internet Assigned Numbers Authority (IANA). WIPO, which has a ccTLD Program, has launched a database portal, facilitating online searches for information related to country code top level domains.

— —

Domain name disputes

What is the nature of domain name disputes?

While designed to serve the function of enabling users to locate computers (and people) in an easy manner, domain names have acquired a further significance as business identifiers and, as such, have come into conflict with the system of business identifiers that existed before the arrival of the Internet and that are protected by intellectual property rights.

Domain name disputes arise largely from the practice of cybersquatting, which involves the pre-emptive registration of trademarks by third parties as domain names. Cybersquatters exploit the first-come, first-served nature of the domain name registration system to register names of trademarks, famous people or businesses with which they have no connection. Since registration of domain names is relatively simple, cybersquatters can register numerous examples of such names as domain names. As the holders of these registrations, cybersquatters often then put the domain names up for auction, or offer them for sale directly to the company or person involved, at prices far beyond the cost of registration. Alternatively, they can keep the registration and use the name of the person or business associated with that domain name to attract business for their own sites.

Domain name disputes in the seven new gTLDs are also subject to the Uniform Domain Name Dispute Resolution Policy (UDRP). In addition, most of these new registry operators have developed, or are in the process of developing, specific dispute resolution policies designed to resolve disputes occurring during a start-up, or "sunrise" phase. WIPO currently administers challenges under these start-up phases for both .info and .biz. Registries that are restricted to certain purposes will also provide special proceedings to resolve disputes concerning compliance with their respective registration restrictions.

Why so many disputes?

There is no agreement within the Internet community that would allow organizations that register domain names to pre-screen the filing of potentially problematic names. The reasons vary, ranging from allowing easy registrations to stimulate business, to the practical difficulties involved in determining who holds the rights to a name, to the principle of freedom of expression. Furthermore, the increasing business value of domain names on the Internet has led to more cybersquatting, which results in more disputes and litigation between the cybersquatters and the businesses or individuals whose names have been registered in bad faith.

How did WIPO get involved in the resolution of disputes?

The Internet grew rapidly over the last decade as a place to do business, although no international legal standards existed to resolve domain name disputes. The Internet Corporation for Assigned Names and Numbers (ICANN), the organization responsible for, among other things, management of the generic top level domains such as .com, .net and .org, was in urgent need of a solution to the dispute resolution problem. The process of negotiating a new international treaty was considered too slow, and new national laws would most likely be too diverse. What was needed were internationally uniform and mandatory procedures to deal with what are frequently cross-border disputes. With the support of its member States, WIPO - which is mandated to promote the protection of intellectual property worldwide - conducted extensive consultations with members of the Internet community around the world, after which it prepared and published a report containing recommendations dealing with domain name issues. Based on the report's recommendations, ICANN adopted the Uniform Domain Name Dispute Resolution Policy (UDRP). The UDRP went into effect on December 1, 1999, for all ICANN-accredited registrars of Internet domain names. Under the UDRP, WIPO is the leading ICANN-accredited domain name dispute resolution service provider. As of the end of 2001, some 60 percent of all the cases filed under the UDRP were filed with WIPO. Additionally, a growing number of registrars of country code top-level domains have designated WIPO as a dispute resolution service provider.

What is the UDRP?

The UDRP is the Uniform Domain Name Dispute Resolution Policy, adopted by the Internet Corporation for Assigned Names and Numbers (ICANN) on August 26, 1999. The UDRP is based on recommendations made by WIPO in the Report on the First WIPO Internet Domain Name Process, focusing on the problems caused by the conflict between trademarks and domain names. A number of further issues identified in that Report that were considered to be outside the scope of the First WIPO Process have been addressed in the subsequent Report of the Second WIPO Internet Domain Name Process.

How does the UDRP work?

In the event that a trademark holder considers that a domain name registration infringes on its trademark, it may initiate a proceeding under the Uniform Domain Name Dispute Resolution Policy (UDRP). Under the standard dispute clause of the Terms and Conditions for the registration of a gTLD domain name, the registrant must submit to such proceedings.

The UDRP permits complainants to file a case with a resolution service provider, specifying, mainly, the domain name in question, the respondent or holder of the domain name, the registrar with whom the domain name was registered and the grounds for the complaint. Such grounds include, as their central criteria, the way in which the domain name is identical or similar to a trademark to which the complainant has rights; why the respondent should be considered as having no rights or legitimate interests in respect of the domain name that is the subject of the complaint; and why the domain name should be considered as having been registered and used in bad faith.

The respondent is offered the opportunity to defend itself against the allegations. The provider (eg: the WIPO Arbitration and Mediation Center) appoints a panelist who decides whether or not the domain(s) should be transfered.

What does WIPO offer as a resolution service provider?

WIPO's resolution service offers highly qualified neutral panelists, thorough and expeditious administrative procedures, and overall impartiality and credibility. Dispute resolution at WIPO is much faster than normal litigation in the courts. A domain name case filed with WIPO is normally concluded within two months, using on-line procedures, whereas litigation can take much longer. Fees are also much lower than normal litigation. There are no in-person hearings, except in extraordinary cases. Minimal filing requirements also help reduce costs. For resolution of a case involving one to five domain names, with a single panelist, the current cost is US$ 1,500; for three panelists, the total cost is US$ 4,000. For six to ten domain names, the current cost is US$ 2,000 for a case involving a sole panelist and US$ 5,000 for a case involving three panelists.

What are the results of the procedures, and are they binding?

A domain name is either transferred or the complaint is denied and the respondent keeps the domain name. It is also possible to seek cancellation of the domain name.

There are no monetary damages applied in UDRP domain name disputes, and no injunctive relief is available. The accredited domain name registrars - which have agreed to abide by the UDRP - implement a decision after a period of ten days, unless the decision is appealed in court in that time. The panel decisions are mandatory in the sense that accredited registrars are bound to take the necessary steps to enforce a decision, such as transferring the name concerned. However, under the UDRP, either party retains the option to take the dispute to a court of competent jurisdiction for independent resolution. In practice, this is a relatively rare occurrence.

What is WIPO doing in addition to administering cases under the UDRP?

The UDRP was originally designed for settling disputes in generic top-level domains such as .com, .net, and .org. However, a number of country code domain name registries also have started to adopt the UDRP or similar policies, and WIPO also provides dispute resolution services for country code top-level domains - for example, .VE for Venezuela and .TV for Tuvalu.

After having addressed trademark issues in the First WIPO Domain Name Process, WIPO has in the Second WIPO Domain Name Process addressed the question of protection for identifiers other than trademarks, such as geographical indications - for wine-producing regions, for example - personal names, trade names, and names or acronyms of international intergovernmental organizations. Developments in the field of domain names and related dispute resolution are extremely dynamic.

- -

Domain name dispute procedures

How do I file a dispute or response?

For the purpose of filing, the majority of parties consult the WIPO filing guidelines, using the WIPO model complaint and the WIPO model response. Parties should familiarize themselves with the Policy and Rules, and the WIPO Supplemental Rules. In addition, to better present their case, parties should consult the decisions of cases that have already been resolved.

How much will it cost and who pays?

The amount due depends on two criteria: the number of domains included in the dispute, and the number of panelists (one or three). The fee consists of an amount to be retained by the Center as an administration fee and an amount to be paid to the panelist(s). In terms of who pays: in the case of a single member panel the fee, in full, is due from the complainant. If it is a three member panel, requested by the complainant, the fee, in full, is due from the complainant. In cases of a three member panel requested by the respondent, the fee is split equally between the complainant and the respondent.

Who makes the decisions and how does WIPO ensure that there is no conflict of interest?

WIPO's role in the dispute process is administrative. It assists the communications between the parties and, taking into account the specific circumstances of each dispute (such as the nationality of the parties and the language of the proceedings) appoints an expert "neutral" or panelist to review the dispute and issue a decision. These panelists are selected from a roster of independent individuals qualified for deciding such cases. Either party to the dispute may opt to have one or three panelists assigned to the case. Panelists must confirm to WIPO the absence of any potential conflict of interest before taking a case, as well as disclose in a written statement any and all facts that should be considered prior to appointment.

What factors guide the panelists' decisions?

The panel decides the case on the base of the criteria, which are cumulative, contained in the UDRP Policy, which also contains practical examples of how a party may prove its compliance with these criteria:

 i. whether the domain name is identical or confusingly similar to a trademark or service mark in which the complainant has rights;

 ii. whether the respondent has any rights or legitimate interests in the domain name (for example, the legitimate offering of goods and services under the same name);

 iii. whether the domain name was registered and is being used in bad faith.

Can damages be awarded?

No. Under the UDRP the panelist can only decide to transfer or cancel the domain name(s), or deny the complaint. It is not possible for the panel to make any monetary judgments.

Are the cases and the decisions posted online?

A list of cases are posted online once WIPO has registered the case. Decisions are posted online as soon as the parties to the dispute have been notified of the decision. It is possible to subscribe to receive daily emails of the new decisions as they are made publicly available. Previous emails listing the decisions are also archived online.

Can I search for a case number, a domain name, a decision or other case-related information online?

It is possible to search all WIPO UDRP cases by domain name or case number, plus use the searchable online Index of the WIPO UDRP decisions. In addition, tabular listings of all cases filed with the WIPO

Arbitration and Mediation Center and all decisions issued by WIPO panels are available. Statistics related to case filing and decisions are updated daily. The Center also makes available an overview of WIPO Panel Views on selected UDRP questions.

Source: http://www.wipo.int/amc/en/center/faq/domains.html

Patents 3

3.1: Introduction to Patent and Types of Patent Applications

The word **Patent** originated from the Latin Word "*Patene*" which means '*to open.*' If a person makes, what he thinks is an invention, he or if he works for an entity, that entity can ask the Government, by filing an application with the Patent Office to give him a certificate in which it is stated what the invention is and that he is the owner of it. Such a right conferred upon the inventor is called 'Patent' by which the inventor, more properly called as the Patentee, can make exclusive use of his invention.

A *Patent* is an intellectual property right relating to inventions and is the grant of exclusive right, for limited period, provided by the Government to the patentee, in exchange of full disclosure of his invention, for excluding others, from making, using, selling, importing the patented product or process producing that product for those purposes. The purpose of this system is to encourage inventions by promoting their protection and utilization so as to contribute to the development of industries, which in turn, contributes to the promotion of technological innovation and to the transfer and dissemination of technology. Under the system, Patents ensure property a right (legal title) for the invention for which patent has been granted, which may be extremely valuable to an individual or a Company. One should make the fullest possible use of the Patent System and the benefits it provides. A patent is a powerful business tool for companies to gain exclusivity over a new product or process, develop a strong market position and earn additional revenues through licensing. A complex product (such as a camera, mobile phone, a car, etc.,) may incorporate a number of inventions that are covered by several patents, which may be owned by different patent holders.

Patent right is territorial in nature and a patent obtained in one country is not enforceable in other country. The inventors/their assignees are required to file separate patent applications in different countries for obtaining the patent in those countries. A patent is granted by the **national patent office** of a country or **a regional patent office** for a group of countries. It is valid for a limited period of time, generally for 20 years from the date of filing of the patent application, provided the required maintenance fees are paid on time. Therefore, the patent is **a territorial right**, limited to the geographical boundary of the relevant country or region.

A patent is an exclusive right granted by a country to the owner of an invention to make, use, manufacture and market the invention, provided the invention satisfies certain conditions stipulated in the law. Exclusivity of right implies that no one else can make, use, manufacture or market the invention without the consent of the patent holder. This right is available only for a limited period of time. However, the use or exploitation of a patent may be affected by other laws of the country, which has awarded the patent.

These laws may relate to health, safety, food, security, etc. Further, existing patents in similar area may also come in the way. A patent in the law is a property right and hence, can be gifted, inherited, assigned, sold or licensed. As the right is conferred by the state, it can be revoked by the state under very special circumstances even if the patent has been sold or licensed or manufactured or marketed in the meantime.

After the expiry of the duration of patent, anybody can make use of the invention. Any person being the inventor of an invention or his assignee can apply alone or jointly with any other person. As per the Indian Patents Act, 1970, invention means any new or useful art, process, method, apparatus or machine. A partnership firm, a private or a public limited company or a corporation can apply for a patent. But they cannot invent and therefore cannot be termed as 'inventor.' Therefore, only individual could be termed as 'inventor.'

Need (Importance of) for Patent System - (Why one should consider Patenting his/her invention?):

The advantages of patent system highlighted with the following points:

1. Patent system encourages an inventor to disclose his invention instead of keeping it secret.

2. Patent gives legal protection to the patentee, enabling his to enjoy the right without any fear of copying and raise the capital for working his invention on a commercial scale.

3. The industries or R&D centres can make use of the technology disclosed in the patent literature as a steeping-stone, avoiding thereby the redundant research, which means "you do not have to reinvent the wheel."

4. it provides an inducement to invest capital in the new lines of production and, thus, provides immense help for development and up-gradation of technology.

5. One may get a very good return through patent right on the investment made in R&D activities.

6. The patent system provides for the strong market position and competitive advantage. Patent system provides a reasonable assurance of working and commercialization of the invention.

7. Patented invention become open to public for free use when it ceases to be in effect.

8. It can act as a stimulant for economic growth by encouraging the foreign investment in joint ventures.

9. It helps to explore unexplored and uncovered areas.

10. Vast patent literature offers an ocean of scientific and technological knowledge and information of the use of public. It encourages the R&D activities by becoming a 'too' for technology transfer.

11. Patent acts as a tradable industrial asset for an enterprise. A strong patent portfolio of the company is an indication of its good economic health.

12. It ensures a higher profit or returns on investment.

13. It helps in generating additional income from licensing or assigning the patent on specified conditions to use.

14. It helps in opening an access to technology through cross-licensing agreements.

15. It helps to have an access to new market. Licensing of patents (or even pending patent application) to others may provide access to new markets, which are otherwise inaccessible. In order to do so, the invention must also be protected in the relevant foreign market(s) also.

16. Diminished risks of infringement and enhanced 'freedom to use.'

17. Enhanced ability to obtain grants and raise funds at a reasonable rate of interest.

18. A powerful tool to take action against imitators and free raiders.

19. Helps to develop a positive image of the enterprise, etc.

Features of Patent Right:

1. Patent is a grant of exclusive right by the government, to the inventor or his assignee, for his disclosed invention, which gives protection against infringement and creates possibility of assigning or licensing of the right.

2. It is granted for a limited period and can be enforced only in the country where it is granted, that means it is 'territorial in nature.'

3. A patented invention can normally be exploited only by the patent holder or by someone else with his authorization.

4. Grant of patent prevents others from exploiting the patented invention. This is referred to as a right to exclude others from making use or selling his invention. The patent rights enable the patentee to take legal action against the person who is exploiting the patented invention without the consent or license from the patentee.

5. The Patent Right enables the inventor to derive material benefit, to which he is entitled, as a reward for his intellectual efforts and compensation for expenses incurred in the research and experimentation relating to his invention.

6. The patentee acquires the right, enforceable by law, to decide who shall and who shall not use his patented invention. He retains this right for the term of the patent provided he pays the necessary renewal fees.

7. The grant of patent right by the government does not mean that the government itself would automatically enforce the patent right. It is up to the owner to bring and action, usually under civil law, for any infringement of his patent right. The patentee must, therefore, be his own 'policeman.'

Feasibility of Applying for Patent:

If an invention is patentable, is it always wise to apply for patent protection?

Not always, if an invention is patentable, it does not necessarily follow that it will result in a commercially viable technology or product. Therefore, a careful weighting of pros and cons and an analysis of possible alternatives is essential before filing a patent application. A patent may be expensive and difficult to obtain, maintain and enforce. To file or not to file a patent application is strictly a business decision. It should be based primarily on the probability of obtaining commercially useful protection for the invention that is likely to provide significant benefits from its eventual business use.

Therefore, the factors to be taken into account in deciding whether or not to file a patent application include:

- Is there a market for the invention?

- What are the alternatives to our invention, and how do they compare with our invention?

- Is the invention useful for improving an existing product or developing a new product? If so, does it fit in with our company's business strategy?

- Are there potential licenses or investors who will be willing to help to take the invention to market?

- How valuable will the invention be to our business and to competitors?

- Is it easy to 'reverse engineer' our invention from our product or 'design around' it?

- How likely are others', especially competitors, to invent and patent what we have been invented?

- Do the expected profits from an exclusive position in the market justify the cost of patenting?

- What aspects of the invention can be protected by one or more patents, how broad can this coverage be and will this provide commercially useful protection?

- Will it be easy to identify violation of the patent rights and are we ready to invest time and financial resources for enforcing our patent(s)?

Conditions to be satisfied by an invention to be patentable:

The question here is to answer – What can be patented?

An invention must meet several requirements to be eligible for patent protection. These include, in particular, that the claimed invention:

- Consist of **patentable subject matter,**

- Is **new** (novelty requirement),

- Involves **an inventive step** (non-obviousness requirement); and

- Is **disclosed** in a clear and complete manner in the patent application (disclosure requirement).

Therefore, an invention means any new and useful:

i. Art, process, method or manner of manufacture,

ii. Machine, apparatus or other article,

iii. Substance produced by manufacture and includes any new & useful improvement of any of them and an alleged invention.

Therefore, in order to be patentable, an invention must possess the following **characteristics**:

a) It should relate to a manner of manufacture.

b) The manner of manufacture should be novel.

c) It should be the outcome of inventive activity.

d) It should have utility.

e) It should not be contrary to law and morality.

What is Patentable Subject Matter?

In most national and regional patent laws, patentable subject matter is defined negatively, i.e., by providing a list of what cannot be patented. While there are considerable differences between countries, the following are the examples of some of the areas may be excluded from patentability.

- Discoveries and scientific theories.

- Aesthetic creations.

- Schemes, rules and methods for performing mental acts.

- Mere discoveries of substance as they naturally occur in the world.

- Inventions that may affect public order, good morals or public health.

- Diagnostic, therapeutic and surgical methods of treatment for humans or animals.

- Plants and animals other than microorganisms, and essential biological process for the production of plants or animals other than non-biological and microbiological processes.

- Computer programs

Inventions claiming substance intended for use, or capable of being used, as food or as medicine or drug or relating to substances prepared or produced by chemical processes (including alloys, optical glass, semiconductors and inter-metallic compounds) are not patentable. Only process claims are allowed in such cases. Meaning of chemical process would also include the biochemical, biotechnological and microbiological process.

[The Indian Patents Act also lays down some norms as to which inventions are not patentable. Following inventions are not patentable:

a) An invention which is frivolous or which claims anything obvious or contrary to well established natural laws.

b) An invention, the primary or intended use of which would be contrary to any law or morality or injurious to public health.

c) The mere discovery of a scientific principle or the formulation of an abstract theory.

d) The mere discovery of any new property or new use for a known substance or of the mere use of a known process, machine or apparatus unless such known process results in a new product or employs atleast one new reactant.

e) A substance obtained by a mere admixture resulting only in the aggregation of the properties of the components thereof or a process for producing such substance.

f) The mere arrangement or rearrangement or duplication of known devices each functioning independently of one another in a known way.

g) A method or process of testing applicable during the process of manufacture for rendering the machine, apparatus or other equipment more efficient or for the improvement or restoration of the existing machine, apparatus or other equipment or for the improvement or control of manufacture.

h) A method of agriculture or horticulture.

i) A process for the medical, surgical, curative, prophylactic or other treatment of human beings or any process for a similar treatment of animals or plants to render them free of disease or to increase their economic value or that of their products.

j) An invention relating to atomic energy.

k) A **computer program** is not considered a patentable invention. It is protected under the Copyright Law but Computer Programs which have the effect of controlling the computers to operate in a particular form are embodied in physical form were held to be patentable. A claim to a process for conditioning the operation of a computer and an associated plotter of known types to produce a layout was held patentable.]

How is an invention judged to be new or novel?

An invention is new or novel if it does not form part of the **prior art (global state-of-the-art)**. In general, prior are refers to all the relevant technical knowledge available to the public anywhere in the world prior to the first filing date of the relevant patent application. It includes, *inter alia*, patents, patent applications and non-patent literature of all kinds.

The definition of prior art differs considerably from country to country. In many countries, any information disclosed to the public anywhere in the world in written form, by oral communication, by display or through public use constitutes prior art. Thus, in principle, the publication of the invention in a scientific journal, magazines, books, newspapers, etc., its use in commerce or its display in a company's catalogue would all constitute acts that could destroy the novelty of the invention (as it constitute the prior art or state-of-the-art) and render it unpatentable. It is important to prevent accidental disclosure of inventions prior to filing the patent application. Prior art often includes 'secret prior art' such as pending unpublished patent applications, provided they are published at a later stage. Prior use of the invention in the country of interest before the filing date can also destroy the novelty. Therefore, the novelty is determined through extensive literature and patent searches. It should be realized that patent search is essential and critical for ascertaining novelty as most of the information reported in patent documents does not get published anywhere else.

When is an invention considered to "involve an inventive step"?

An invention is considered to involve an **inventive step (non-obvious)** when, taking into account the prior art, the invention would not have been obvious to a person skilled in the particular field of technology. The non-obviousness requirement is meant to ensure that patents are only granted in respect of truly creative and inventive achievements, and not to developments that a person with ordinary skill in the field could easily deduce from what already exists. The invention thus should be technically advanced enhancing the science.

The complexity or the simplicity of an inventive step does not have any bearing on the grant of a patent. In other words, a very simple invention can qualify for a patent. If there is an inventive step between the proposed patent and the prior art at that point of time, then an invention has taken place. A mere 'scintilla' of invention is sufficient to found a valid patent.

Some of the examples of what may not qualify as inventive, as established by past court decisions in some countries are: mere change of size, making a product portable, the reversal of parts, the change of materials, or the mere substitution by an equivalent part or function.

What is meant by "Capable of Industrial Application"?

It means that the invention is capable of being made or used in an industry. To be patentable, an invention must be capable of being used for an industrial or business purpose. An invention cannot be mere theoretical phenomenon; it must be useful and provide some practical benefit. The term 'industrial' is meant here in the broadest sense as anything distinct from purely intellectual or aesthetic activity, and includes, for example, agriculture. In some countries, instead of industrial applicability, the criterion is utility.

What is the Disclosure requirement?

According to the national legislation in most of the countries, **a patent application must disclose the invention** in a manner sufficiently clear and complete for the invention to be carried out by a person skilled in the specific technical field. In some countries, patent law requires that the inventor discloses the "best mode" for practicing the invention. For patents involving microorganisms, many countries require the microorganism to be deposited at a recognized **depositary** institution.

Who is an Inventor and who owns the rights over a Patent?

The person who conceived the invention is the **inventor**, whereas the person (or company) that files the patent application is the **applicant, holder** or **owner** of the patent. While in some cases the inventor may also be the applicant, the two are often different entities; the applicant is often the company or research institution that employs the inventor. The following specific circumstances merit further analysis:

- **Employee Invention**: In many countries, inventions developed in the course of employment are automatically assigned to the employer. In some countries, this is only so if it is so stated in the employment contract. In some cases (e.g., if there is no employment agreement) the inventor may retain the right to exploit the invention, but the employer is given a non-exclusive right to use the invention for its internal purposes (called 'shop rights'). It is important to find out about the specific legislation in one's own country and to ensure that employment contracts deal with issues of ownership over employee inventions to avoid future disputes.

- **Independent Contractors**: In most of the countries, an independent contractor hired by a company to develop a new product or process owns all rights to the invention, unless specifically stated otherwise. This means that, unless the contractor has written agreement with the company, in general, the company will have no ownership rights in what is developed, even if it paid for the development.

- **Joint Inventors**: When more than one person contributes in significant ways to the conception and realization of an invention, they must be treated as joint inventors and mentioned as such in the patent application. If the joint inventors are also the applicants, the patent will be granted to them jointly.

- **Joint Owners**: Different countries and institutions have different rules concerning the exploitation or enforcement of patents that are owned by more than one entity or person. In some cases, no single co-owner may license a patent or sue third parties for infringement without the consent of all other co-owners.

Who owns It: First-to-File or First-to-Invent

In most of the countries, patents are granted to the **first person to file a patent application** on an invention. However, the USA is an exception, where a **first-to-invent** system applies, in which, in case of similar patent applications filed, the patent will be granted to the first inventor who conceived and reduced the invention to practice whether or not the patent application has been filed first. In order to prove inventorship within a first-to-invent system, it is crucial to have well-kept, duly signed and dated laboratory notebooks and other justifiable records, which may be used as evidence in case of a dispute with another company or inventor.

Types of Patent Application:

Following are the major types of patent application:

1. Ordinary Application,
2. Convention Application,
3. PCT International Application,
4. PCT National Phase Application,
5. Application for Patent Addition; and
6. Divisional Application.

1. Ordinary Application:

An application for patent filed in the Patent Office without claiming any priority of application made in a convention country or without any reference to any other application under process in the office is called an ordinary application. An ordinary application must be accompanied with a complete specification and claims.

2. Convention Application:

An application for patent filed in the Patent Office, claiming a priority date based on the same or substantially similar application filed in one or more of the convention countries is called a convention application (by virtue of Paris Convention).

As far as India is concerned, in order to get convention status, an applicant should file the application in the Indian Patent Office within 12 months from the date of first filing of a similar application in the convention country. The priority document and its English translation (if required) also should be submitted by the applicant. A convention application should be accompanied by a complete specification. When two or more applications for patents constituting one invention have been made in one or more convention countries, one application may be made within twelve months from the date on which the earlier or earliest of those applications was made. Multiple fees have to be remitted for multiple priorities so that the other applications filed earlier in the convention countries will be deemed to have been published in India. The applicant of convention application shall furnish when required by the Controller, copies of specification or documents (priority documents) certified by the official chief of the patent office of the convention country. If any such specification or document is in a foreign language, a translation into English of the specification or document shall be furnished.

3. PCT International Application:

A PCT Application is an international application governed by the Patent Cooperation Treaty, and can be validated in upto 142 countries. The Patent Cooperation Treaty or PCT is an international agreement for filing patent applications. However, there is nothing called as a 'world patent.' The PCT application does not provide for the grant of an international patent, it simply provides a streamlined process for the patent application process in many countries at the same time.

Advantages of filing a PCT Application

- A single international patent application can be filed in order to seek protection for an invention in up to 142 countries throughout the world.

- The priority date obtained by filing a PCT application is internationally recognized, and has an effect in each of the countries designated.

- It gives the application 30 to 31 months to enter into various countries from the international filing date or the priority date, and therefore gives the applicant more time to assess the viability of the invention.

- Delays the expenses associated with applying for a patent in various countries

- Provides an International Search Report citing prior art, which gives an indication to the applicant whether the invention is novel and innovative.

- Provides an option for requesting an International Preliminary Examination Report, the report containing an opinion on the patentability of the invention.

- The International Search Report and International Preliminary Examination Report, allows the applicant to make more informed choices early in the patent process, and to amend the application to deal with any conflicting material, before the major expenses of the national phase of the patent process begin. It also gives the applicant a fair idea on the patentability of the invention before incurring charges for filing and prosecuting the application in each country.

4. PCT National Phase Application:

The PCT-national phase must follow the international phase. The applicant must individually 'enter into the national phase.' i.e. file a National phase application in each county he wishes to enter. The applicant can enter the national phase in up to 138 countries within 30–31 months (depends on the laws of the designated countries) from the international filing date or priority date (whichever is earlier). If the applicant does not enter the national phase within the prescribed time limit, the International Application loses its effect in the designated or elected States. [*When an international application is made according to PCT designating India, an applicant can file the national phase application in India within 31 months from the international filing date or the priority date (whichever is earlier)*].

5. Application for Patent Addition:

When an applicant feels that he has come across an invention which is a slight modification or improvement of the invention for which he has already applied for or has obtained patent, the applicant can go for patent of addition if the invention does not involve a substantial inventive step. There is no need to pay separate renewal fee for the patent of addition during the term of the main patent and it expires along with the main patent.

6. Divisional Application:

When an application made by applicant claims more than one invention, the applicant on his own or to meet the official objection may divide the application and file two or more applications, as applicable for each of the inventions. This type of application, divided out of the parent one, is called a Divisional Application The priority date for all the divisional applications will be same as that claimed by the Parent Application (Ante-dating).

3.2: Patent Specifications

A Patent Specification is a document describing the invention for which patent is sought and setting out the scope of the protection of the patent. The patent specification filed along with the patent application consists of detailed proceeding about the invention. It is very important document as it determines patentability of an invention; it contains all the disclosure of the invention. It has all the technical aspect of the invention and provides scientific explanation for the same. The specification is a legal document as it contains the right of the patentee and the content of the specifications are susceptible to interpretation by the Courts of Law.

Each patent office has rules relating to the form of the specification, defining such things as paper size, font, layout, section ordering and headings. Such requirements vary between offices. A description cannot generally be modified once it is filed (with narrow exceptions), so it is important to have it done correctly the first time.

There are two kinds of specifications:

1. Provisional Specification
2. Complete Specification

1. Provisional Specification:

The Provisional Specification involves the nature of invention and the process involved in the proposed invention. This basically helps to establish the identity of the invention and registers the earliest authorship of an invention in the patent office. In other words, a provisional specification is usually filed to establish priority of the invention in case the disclosed invention is only at a conceptual stage and a delay is expected in submitting full and specific description of the invention. Although, a patent application accompanied with provisional specification doesn't confer any legal patent rights to the applicants, it is, however, a very important document to establish the earliest ownership (authorship) of an invention. Provisional specification is a permanent and independent scientific-cum-legal document and no amendment is allowed in this. No patent is granted on the basis of a provisional specification. It has to be followed by a complete specification for obtaining a patent for the said invention. Complete specification must be submitted with in 12 months of filing the provisional specification. This period can be extended by 3 months. However, it is not necessary to file an application with provisional specification before the complete specification. An application with complete specification can be filed right at the first instance.

2. Complete Specification:

The Complete Specification is filed after the Provisional Specification and is a more detailed document. To be more precise a complete specification must be furnished with greater details and more accuracy. A Complete Specification may consist of identical description which has been already furnished in provisional specification and the two are permanent independent document. The complete specification must describe the claimed invention and the technical information contained in it with enough details so as to enable anyone who is skilled in the same technical field could make the invention without any further inventive steps.

Following are the major *parts/contents* of the Complete Specification:

a) Title – There should be a title to the specification which must be concise but illustrative in itself.

b) The Opening Description – It is more illustrative than title and provides preamble to the invention.

c) Prior-Art Reference and the Background of the invention – This aspect deals with the previous knowledge of the present invention and all disclosure in this regard. The background of the invention helps in understanding the drawback associated with known art. In India the applicant is not required to provide any prior-art reference.

d) Object of the Invention – For the patentability of the invention the utility aspects must be clearly laid. Therefore, the actual purpose of the invention with its objectives must be specified.

e) Statement of Invention – If the applicant adds one or more omnibus claims at the end of the claims than he should provide supporting statement of invention which is in verbal agreement with the main claim.

f) Detailed Description of the Invention – This part contains illustrative explanation with all pros and consequences of the invention. The description should be sufficient enough to enable the notional skilled person to put the invention into practice. In case of biological invention, it is required to mention the source or geographical origin of biological material used for the invention.

g) Brief description of the Drawings, if necessary.

h) Claim – It defines the monopoly right and the patentee is under a statutory obligation to state in the claims clearly and distinctly what is the invention which he desire to protect. The claims determine the patentability and scope of the claimed invention. A set of properly drafted claims is an important part of complete specification. The Complete Specification must have one claim. The subsidiary claims refer to the main claim and include qualifying or explanatory clauses on the various integers of the main claim or optional features. They may also contain independent claims. Although, the claim-clauses consist of a number of claims, the totality of the claims must relate to one invention only. It should be noted that a claim is a statement of technical facts expressed in legal terms defining the scope of the invention sought to be protected. In patent litigation, interpreting the claims is the first step in determining whether the patent has been infringed.

i) Abstract (Summary) – it is the concise summary of the invention preferably within 150 words and shall commence with the title of the invention. The abstract should be prepared in such a way that one can understand the technical problem and solution with its usefulness.

Under Indian Patents Act Section 9 deals with Provisional and Complete Specification which is laid as under:

- Where an application for patent (not being convention application) is accompanied by a provisional specification, a complete specification shall be filed with 12 months from the date of filing of the application, and if the complete specification is not so filed the application shall be deemed to be abandoned. Provided that the complete specification may be filed at any time after 12 months but within 15 months from the date aforesaid, if a request to that effect is made to the Controller and the prescribed fee is paid on or before the date on which the complete specification is filed.

- Where two or more application in the name of the same applicant are accompanied by provisional specifications in respect of inventions which are cognate of which one is a modification of another and the Controller may allow one complete specification to be filed in respect of all such provisional specifications.

- Where an application for a patent (not being a convention application) is accompanied by a specification purporting to be a complete specification, the Controller my, if the applicant so request at any time before the acceptance of the specification, direct that such specification shall be treated for the purposes of this Act as a provisional specification and proceed with the application accordingly.

- Where a complete specification has been filed in pursuance of an application for a patent accompanied by a provisional specification or by a specification treated by virtue of a direction under sub-section (3) as a provisional specification, the Controller may, if the applicant so request at any time before the acceptance of the complete specification, cancel the provisional specification and post-date the application to the date of filing of the complete specification.

3.3: Patent Filing and Examinations

National and PCT filing Procedure:

National Filing Procedure:

The National filling procedure and the time frame of filing national patent application (with special reference to India) involve the following stages:

- Any person who is true and first inventor or his assignee or legal representative is entitled to apply for a patent either alone or jointly with other persons to protect his invention through patent rights.

- The applicant can file either the provisional or complete specification. The complete specification should be filed within **12 months** after the date of filing the provisional specification.

- Patent Office accords an application number and filing date to the application immediately after filing by the applicant.

- According to the provisions of the Patent (Amendment) Act, 2002 an application shall not be open to the public for a period of **18 months** from the date of filing or date or priority whichever is earlier.

- Except when a secrecy direction is given, every application shall be published on the expiry of **18 months** period.

- Patent applications are published in the "**Patent Office Journal**" under Section 11A(2) of the Patents (Amendment) Act, 2005 and Rule 24 A of the Patents (Amendment) Rules, 2005 (before 2005, it used to publish in Gazette of India, Part III, Section 2).

- The application shall be examined only after receiving a Request for Examination either from the applicant or any interest person, in a prescribed manner within 36 months from the date of filing of the application or from the date of priority whichever is earlier.

- If the Request for Examination is not made within the stipulated period, the application shall be treated as withdrawn by the applicant.

- All the applications are screened and provided international classification to categories the invention to the respective field or technology.

- The Examiner will conduct a search for novelty, using the databases and literature available.

- The technical and legal defects observed by the Examiner in the complete specification are submitted to the Controller in the form of objections for his approval

- A statement of objections, the "First Examination Report" (FER), is issued to the applicant by the Patent Office. The applicant shall submit his first reply to FER within **6 months** of the date of issue of FER.

- The applicant shall rectify all the legal and technical defects and put the application in order for acceptance within a period of **12 months**.

- The application can be opposed on various grounds laid down in the Patent Act. If the application is not opposed, the patent shall be granted as expeditiously and as possible to the applicant or, in the case of joint application, to the applicants jointly with the seal of the Patent Office and the date on which the patent is granted shall be entered in the register.

- In order to keep the patent in force, renewal fee is to be paid in the Patent Office annually.

- The purpose of grant of patent in India is that the invention should be exploited by the way of manufacturing the patented product in India. Every patentee should furnish periodical statement as to the extent to which patented invention has been worked on a commercial basis in India.

PCT filing Procedure:

The PCT provides at least 18 additional months on to of 12 months priority period, in which applicants can explore the commercial potential of their product or invention in various countries and decide where to seek patent protection. Payment of the fees and translation costs associated with national application is thus delayed. The PCT is widely used by applicants to keep their options open for as long as possible.

PCT applicants receive valuable information about the potential patentability of their invention in the form of the PCT International Search Report (ISR) and the written opinion of the International Searching Authority (ISA). These documents provide PCT applicants with a strong basis on which they can make their decisions about whether and where to pursue patent protection.

The International Search Report (ISR) contains a list of prior art documents from all over the world, which have been identified as relevant to the invention. The Written Opinion of the International Searching Authority (ISA) analyzes the potential patentability in the light of the results of the International Search Report (ISR).

A single PCT application, in one language and with one se of fees, has legal effect in all PCT member countries. This effect significantly reduces the initial transaction costs of submitting separate application to each patient office. The PCT may also be used to file applications under some of the regional patent systems. A brief outline of the PCT application process is given below:

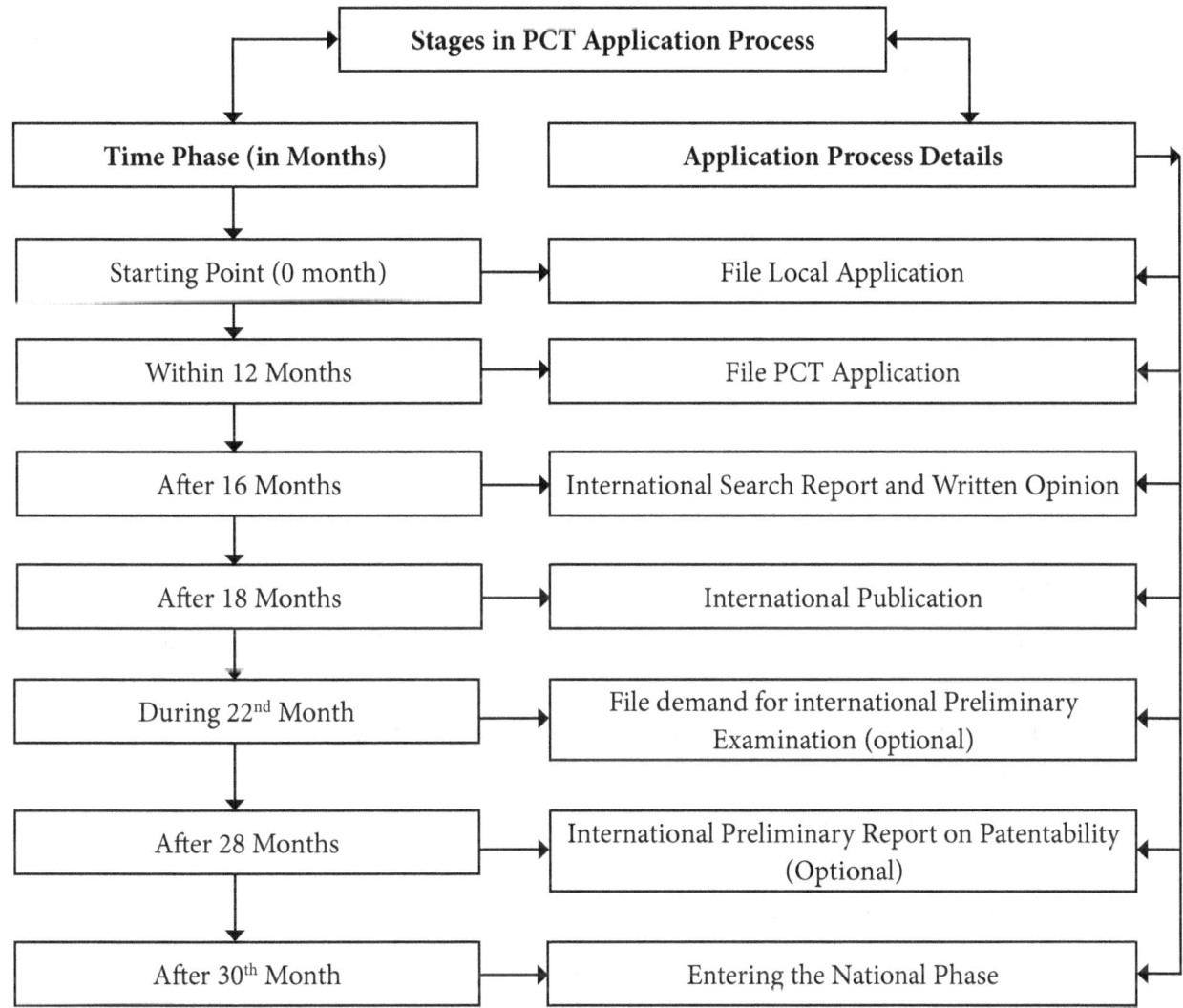

Schedule of Charges in PCT Filing Procedure:

SL No.	DESCRIPTION OF SERVICES	ATTORNEY FEE US$	OFFICIAL FEE US$ - For natural person	OFFICIAL FEE US$ - For others
1	Filing PCT National Phase application upto 30 pages having upto 10 claims:-	500	23	89
	i.for each sheet of specification in addition to 30	10	3	9

(Contd.)

SL No.	DESCRIPTION OF SERVICES	ATTORNEY FEE US$	OFFICIAL FEE US$ - For natural person	OFFICIAL FEE US$ - For others
	ii.for each claim in addition to 10	10	5	18
2	For claiming priority (per priority).	50	23	89
3	Filing Request for Publication u/s.11A(2)	200	56	312
4	Filing Request for Examination.	200	78	223
5	Filing Request for extension of time.	50	7 (per month)	27 (per month)
6	Filing Request for amending the name/ address/representative for service.	100	5	18
7	Application for amendment of patent/ complete specification:			
	i. Before acceptance	100	12	45
	ii. After acceptance	100	23	89
8	Reporting Official Action, considering instructions and filing response.	200	Nil	Nil
9	Conducting search by name/subject matter of the patent.	250	Nil	Nil
10	Paying an annuity -			
	i. Each year from the 2nd year to the 5th year.	100	12	45
	ii. Each year from the 6th year to the 10th year.	100	33	134
	iii. Each year from the 10th year to the 15th year.	100	67	267
	iv. Each year from the 15th year to the 20th year.	100	112	445

Steps or Stages in patenting:

The grant of patent assures the protection to the inventor for his invention. Thus when a monopoly right is given, it should follow a proper statutory track. Following are the generally accepted (including India) procedure to ensure the monopoly right to the inventor.

The patent procedure consists of the following **four major steps or stages:**

1) **Application for the Patent** – i.e., the filing of the patent application

2) **Examination and Acceptance of the Patent Application**

3) **Opposition to the Grant of Patent** – i.e., advertisement in the Official Gazette and opposition proceedings, if any (within 4 months from the date of advertisement)

4) **Grant and Sealing of Patent** - (the whole process will complete with the period of 4 to 5 years)

1. Application for the Patent:

Application is required to be filed according to the territorial limits where the applicant or the first mentioned applicant in case of joint applicants for a patent normally resides, or has domicile or has a place of business, or the place from where the invention actually originated.

Under Indian Patent Act, 1970 an applicant who claims to be true and first inventor or the legal representative of the same can file an application for the patent. If an assignee files an application he has to furnish evidence of assignment of right to apply for a patent in his favour before making such application. Here under application must be made in the name of true and first inventor. Application for Patent includes the following parts:

- filing of form under section - 7
- filing of specifications under section - 9
- priority search documents
- publication of application

Documents required for filing patent application:

a) Application form in triplicate (Form 1).

b) Provisional and complete specification in triplicate (Form 2). If the provisional specification is filed it must be followed by complete specification within 12 months (15 months with extension).

c) Drawing in triplicate (if necessary).

d) Abstract of the invention in triplicate.

e) Information and undertaking listing the number, filing date and current status of each foreign patent application in duplicate (Form 3).

f) Priority document (if priority date is claimed) in convention application, when directed by the Controller.

g) Declaration of the inventorship where provisional specification is followed by complete specification or in case of convention application or PCT national phase application (Form 5).

h) Power of attorney (if filed through Patent Agent).

i) Fee payable in cash or by local cheque or by demand draft. It is to be noted that the cheque or demand draft should be payable to the "Controller of Patents" drawn on any schedule bank at a place where the appropriate office is situated.

Withdrawal of Patent Application:

The application for patent can be withdrawn at least **03 months** before the first publication which will be **18 months** from the date of filing or date of priority whichever is earlier.

The application can also be withdrawn at any time before the grant of patent. The application withdrawn after the date of publication cannot be refilled as it is already laid open for public inspection. However, application withdrawn before the publication can be refilled provided it is not opened to public otherwise.

Publication of the Application:

The application of the patent shall not be put forth in front of public for 18 months. The time period of 18 months shall be examined from the date of filing the patent application or the prior date which ever is earlier. This publication shall always be notified in Official Gazette or Patent Office Journals. The publication of application includes particulars of:

- date of application
- number of application
- name and address of the applicant identifying the application
- an abstract which is laid in Section IIA of the Patent (Amendment) Act, 2002 .

The applicant may also file a request for early publication in Form – 9 with a prescribed fee of Rs.2,500 for natural person and Rs. 10,000 for other than natural person. Then the application is published ordinarily within one month from the date of the request on Form – 9. The applicant shall have provisional rights from the date of publication.

2) Examination and Acceptance of the Patent Application:

After the completion of filing of application there will be examination of application, which consists of

- Request for Examination
- Final Examination

No application for patent will be examined if no request is made by the applicant or by any other interested person in Form – 18 with prescribed fee with in a period of 48 months from the date of priority of the application or from the date of filing of the application, whichever is earlier. Where no request for examination of the application for patent has been filed within the prescribed period, the aforesaid application will be treated as withdrawn and, thereafter, application cannot be revived.

Application for patent, where request has been made by the applicant or by any other interested person, will be taken up for examination, according to the serial number of the requests received on Form – 18. A First Examination Report (FER) stating the objections/requirements is communicated to the applicant or his agent according to the address for service ordinarily within 06 months from the date of request for examination or date of publication, whichever is later. Application or complete specification should be amended in order to meet the objections/requirements within a period of 12 months from the date of First Examination Report (FER). No further extension of time is available in this regard. If all the objections are not complied with within the period of 12 months, the application shall be deemed to have been abandoned. When all the requirements are met the patent is granted, the letter of patent is issued, entry is made in the register of patents and it is notified in the Patent Office Journal.

3) Opposition to the Grant of Patent:

The opposition can be raised by any interested person may be in the form of

a) Pre-grant Opposition; and

b) Post Grant Opposition.

a) The Pre-Grant Opposition:

Any person interested in opposition for grant of the patent may give the notice of the Controller within four months from the date of advertisement of acceptance of a complete specification (i.e., the application for a patent has been published but has not been granted) under patent Act. However, an extension of one month is possible; a request for extension has to be made within the first four months. The representation of the opposition shall be filed at the appropriate office and shall include a statement and evidence, if any, in support of the representation and a request for hearing, if so desired.

The opponents can base opposition within the limits of Section - 25 (cannot raised any other ground for opposition else than Section – 25). The grounds available for opposition are:

- Obtaining the invention and claims wrongfully
- Prior publication
- Prior claim in a concurrent application
- Prior public use and knowledge (traditional knowledge)
- Obviousness and lack of inventive step
- Non-patentable invention
- Insufficient description of the invention
- Failure to disclose information relating to foreign application
- If convention application, not made within the prescribed time.

b) Post Grant Opposition:

Any interested person can file notice of opposition (along with written statement and evidence, if any) anytime after the grant of patent but before the expiry of a period of one year from the date of publication of grant of a patent in the Patent Office Journal. The above notice under Section - 25(2) shall be filed on Form – 7 along with a fee of Rs. 1,500 for natural person and Rs. 6,000 for other than natural person, in duplicate at the appropriate office. The grounds of opposition under Section - 25(2) are the same as given in the case of pre-grant opposition (as stated in Section – 25). The post grant opposition is decided by an Opposition Board followed by a hearing and the reasoned decision by the Controller.

4) Grant and Sealing of Patent:

The last and final step is the grant of the patent and sealing. Section – 43 of the Act deals with grant and sealing of patent and empowers the Controller to grant and seal the patent. When all the requirements of the FER are met or in case of opposition under Section – 25, if the opposition is decided in favour of the applicant, the patent is granted, after **06 months** from the date of publication (however, where at the expiration of the said period of six months any proceedings in relation to the application for the patent is pending before the Controller or the Appellate Board, the request my be made within the prescribed period after the final determination of the proceeding; where the applicant has died before the expiration of the time within which the request could be otherwise be made anytime within 12 months after the death or as the Controller may think fit) under Section 11A, the letter of patent is issued, entry is made in the register of patents and it is notified in the Patent Office Journal, thereafter opening the application, specification and other related documents for public inspection on payment of prescribed fee.

To keep the patent in force, renewal fee is to be paid every year. The first renewal fee is payable for the third year and must be paid before the expiration of the second year from the date of patent. If the patent has not been granted within two years, the renewal fees my be accumulated and paid immediately after the patent is granted, or within three months of it's recording in the Register of Patents or within an extended period of 09 months, by paying extension fees of six months on Form – 4, from the date of recoding in the register of patents. If the renewal fee is not paid within the prescribed time, the patent will cease to have effect. However, a provision to restore the patent is possible provided application is made with in **18 months** from the date of cessation. No renewal fees is payable on Patents of Addition, unless the original patent is revoked and if the Patent of Addition is converted into an independent patent; renewal fee, then, becomes payable for the remainder of the term of the main patent.

Facts pertaining to Patenting:

General precautions for Applicant while Patent Filing:

The first to file system is employed, in which, among persons having filed the same invention, first one is granted; therefore, a patent application should be filed promptly after conceiving the invention. It is common experience that being ignorant of patent law, inventors act unknowingly and jeopardize the chance of obtaining patents for their invention. Most common mistakes in this regard is to publish their invention in newspapers or scientific and technical journals, before applying for patents. Publication of an invention, even by the inventor himself, would except under certain rare circumstances) constitute evidence to destroy the novelty or patentability of the invention subsequently. Similarly, the use of invention in public, or the commercial use of the invention, prior to the date of filing patent application would be a fatal objection to the grant of a patent for such invention thereafter. There is, however, no objection to the secret working of the invention by way of reasonable trial or experiment, or to the disclosure of the invention to others, confidentially.

Another mistake, which is frequently committed by the inventors, is to wait until their inventions are fully developed for commercial working, before applying for patents. It is, therefore, advisable to apply for a patent as soon as the inventor's idea of the nature of the invention has taken a definite shape filing a provisional specification describing the invention to acquire a priority date.

Therefore, it is advisable to the inventor to consider the following **aspects as precautions** while filing a patent application:

- priority date and prior art
- to be the first to file
- non-disclosure
- timely filing the provisional and complete specifications,
- prompt filing of the application,
- patent search,
- working of the invention,
- provisional and complete specifications, etc.

Patenting Abroad:

Why apply for patents abroad?

Patents are territorial rights, which means than an invention is only protected in the countries or regions where patent protection has been obtained. In other words, if an inventor has not been granted a patent with effect in a given country, his/her invention will not be protected in that country, enabling anybody else to make, use, import or sell the inventors invention in that country.

Patent protection in foreign countries will enable the inventor or the company to enjoy exclusive rights over the patented invention in those countries. Moreover, it may enable the inventor or the company to license the invention to foreign firms, develop outsourcing relationship, and accesses those markets in partnership with others.

Where should the inventor protect the invention?

As protecting an invention in many countries is an expensive undertaking, the inventor or the companies should carefully select the countries in which they require protection. Some of the key consideration when selecting where to patent are:

- Where is the patented product likely to be commercialized?
- Which are the main markets for similar products?
- What are the costs involved in patenting in each target market and what is the budget available with the inventor or the companies?
- Where will the product be manufactured?
- How difficult will it be to enforce a patent in a given country?

Three ways or route to apply for patent protection abroad

(How do inventors or the companies apply for patent protection abroad?)

There are three main ways of patenting an invention abroad:

i. the national route

ii. the regional route

iii. the international route (through PCT application)

i) The National Route: The inventor may apply to the national patent office of each country of interest, by filing a patent application in the required language and paying the required fees. This path may be very cumbersome and expensive, if number of countries is large.

ii) The Regional Route: When a number of countries are members of a regional patent system, the inventor or the companies may apply for protection, with effect in the territories of all or some of these, by filing an application at the relevant regional office. The regional patent offices are:

- The African Intellectual Property Organization (OAPI)
- The African Regional Intellectual Property Organization (ARIPO)
- The Eurasian Patent Organization (EAPO)
- The European Patent Office (EPO)
- The Patent Office of the Gulf Cooperation Council, etc.

iii) The International Route: If the inventor or the companies want to have the option of protecting an invention in any number of member countries of the Patent Cooperation Treaty (PCT), then the inventor or the companies should consider filing an international PCT application. To be eligible to do so, the inventor or the companies must be a national or resident of a PCT Contracting State, or, the inventor's or the companies' business must have a real and effective industrial or commercial presence in one of these countries. By filing one international application under the PCT, the inventor or the companies may simultaneously seek patent protection for an invention in the more than 142 member countries of the PCT. This application may be filed either at inventor's national or regional patent office and/or at the PCT receiving office at eh World Intellectual Property Organization's office (WIPO's office) in Geneva, Switzerland.

3.4: Patent Search and Databases

Conducting patent searches is very useful for several purposes, not only for organizations such as SMEs and Universities, but also for A variety of people, such as inventors, historians, lawyers, students, educators, government agencies, and engineers. Indeed, patents include both technical and legal information and can consequently be used to:

Patentability: Conduct a preliminary patent search to assess novelty of an invention. Research and Development: Evaluate a technology, develop new – or improve upon existing –products and processes.

Technical: Solve specific problems, locate sources of expertise, and identify alternate technology.

Economic: Survey markets, monitor and forecast activities of competitors or industries.

Financial: Avoid duplicating costly research; judge an alleged innovation prior to venturing capital.

Legal: Conduct infringement or opposition proceedings; identify licensing opportunities.

Historical: Study a time period, the history of technology, or social changes.

Educational: Research thesis or science projects, pursue scientific academic programs and studies, and teach inventive and creative thinking skills.

Marketing: Compile mailing lists and databases;locate the addresses of inventors or manufacturers.

Genealogy: Research and document family ancestors and accomplishments.

(Source: Patents: The Collection for All Reasons, Patent and Trademark Depository Library Program, http://www.uspto.gov/go/ptdl/patreaso.htm.)

Types of patent search

- Theme search

Theme searches provide the overview of patents related to your field of interest. These searches are helpful to detect the recent trend of your technology area and to establish your R&D direction.

- Patentibility search

Patentability search is the first step of patenting process. A patentability search surveys patents filed in each national intellectual property office to check whether there exists inventions similar to yours.

- Infringement search

Infringement search is to check whether patents which can be infringed by your product launched newly in a certain country exist or not in that country.

- Invalidity search

When you intend to make some claims of a particular patent invalid, the invalid search can provide some prior art references that disclose claims that are infringed by the subject disclosure.

- Family patent/legal status search

Patent family search provide a list of all countries in which a particular patent was filed. Legal status search gives the legal progressing status of a particular patent.

Patent searching process

A) Searching by patent attributes

- ➢ By subject – assume most common

- ➢ Patent title, number

- ➢ Inventor

- ➢ Date of invention

- ➢ Country of origin

B) Constructing a keyword search: generate & list terms

- ➢ What is known about the invention?

- ➢ Function

- ➢ Describe what it does in as many ways as possible; use synonyms

- ➢ Structure

- ➢ What parts compose it?

- ➢ Electrical?

- ➢ Structural and chemical forms: steel, silicon,etc

- ➢ Chemical reactions? What are end products?

C) Expand on terms:

Boolean logic

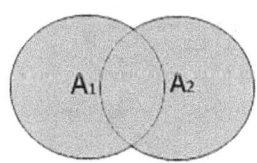

A1 OR A2

{IDEA A(1) TERM(S)} **OR** {IDEA A(2) TERM(S)} OR Retrieves all records including either term. – **usually used to connect synonyms in a search Example: column OR pillar**

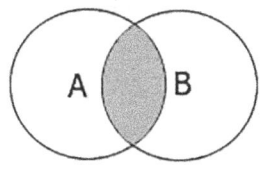

A AND B

{IDEA A TERM(S)} **AND** {IDEA B TERM(S)} AND Retrieves only those records containing both terms.– **usually used for contrasting terms in a search Example: brittle AND elastic**

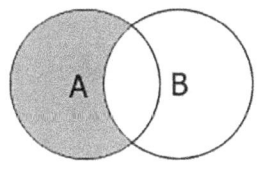

A NOT B

{IDEA A TERM(S)} **NOT** {IDEA B TERM(S)}NOT Excludes records containing a particular term.

Example: brittle NOT elastic

Following are the free online databases for the patent search

- ✓ Kipris.or.kr
- ✓ Uspto.gov
- ✓ Espacenet.com
- ✓ Ipdl.jpo.go.jp
- ✓ sipo.gov.cn

3.5: Commercializing Patent Technology

A patent on its own is no guarantee of commercial success. It is a tool that enhances a company's capacity to benefit from its inventions. In order to provide a tangible benefit to a company, a patent needs to be exploited effectively and will generally make money only if the product based on the patent is successful in the market or boosts the firm's reputation and bargaining power. To take a patented invention to market, a company has a range of options:

- Commercializing the patented invention directly
- Selling the patent to someone else
- Licensing the patent to others
- Stabling a joint venture or other strategic alliance with others having complementary assets.

Licensing Patent:

A patent is licensed when the owner of the patent (the licensor) grants permission to another (the licensee) to use the patented invention for mutually agreed purposes. In such cases, a **licensing contract (licensing agreement)** is generally signed between the two parties, specifying the terms and scope of the agreement.

Authorizing others to commercialize the inventor's patented invention through a licensing agreement will enable the business to obtain an **additional source of revenue** and is a common means of exploiting a company's exclusive rights over an invention.

Licensing is particularly useful if the company that owns the invention is not in a position to make the product at all or in sufficient quantity to meet a given market need, or to cover a given geographical area.

As a license agreement requires skillful negotiations and drafting, it is advisable to seek the assistance of a licensing agreement. In some countries, licensing agreements need to be registered with a government regulatory authority.

In licensing deals, the owner of the right is generally remunerated through lump-sum payments and/ or through recurring royalties, which may be based on sales volume of the licensed product (per unit royalty) or on net sales (net sales-based royalty). In many cases, the remuneration for a patent license is a combination of a lump-sum payment and royalties. Sometimes, an equity state in the company of the license may replace a royalty.

There are three types of licensing agreements depending on the number of licenses that will be allowed to work the patent:

a) Exclusive License: A single licensee has the right to use the patented technology, which cannot even be used by the patent owner.

b) Sole License: A single licensee and the patent owner have the right to use the patented technology; and

c) Non-exclusive license: Several licensees and the patent owner have the right to use the patented technology.

d) Cross Licensing: It may not always be easy or affordable to obtain authorization to incorporate technology owned by a competitor into your products/processes. However, if your competitor is also interested in your company's patents, then you should think of 'cross-licensing.' Cross-licensing is very common in industries where a number of patents covering a wide range of complementary inventions are held by two or more competitors. Such competing companies seek to ensure their 'freedom to operate' by obtaining the right to use patents owned by their competitors while providing the right to use their own patents to the competitors.

In a single licensing agreement, there may be provisions that grant some rights on an exclusive basis and others on a sole or non exclusive basis.

Compulsory Licensing:

Compulsory Licensing is different from the ordinary licensing. The Patents Acts contains definite provision for providing compulsory license. The reason for providing such license in India is obvious from the fact that patents are granted to encourage invention. They are not granted merely to enable the patentee to enjoy a monopoly for the importation of the patented article. The major reasons for the Compulsory Licensing are:

• The patent system has to ensure that the inventions are worked on a commercial.

• The patentee is expected to work the invention in the public and to make available the patented product to the public, that too at a reasonable price and without much delay. (In fields related to socio-economic and technological development, especially relating to public health, the Government has to make sure that the patented products are accessible to the general public at a reasonable price.

Section – 84 of the Indian Patent Act deal with compulsory license which is given below:

a) At any time after the expiration of **three years** from the date of the sealing of a patent, any person interested may make an application to the Controller for grant of compulsory license on patent on any of the following grounds, namely

   ✓ that the reasonable requirements of the public with respect to the patented invention have not been satisfied, or

   ✓ that the patented invention is not available to the public at a reasonably affordable price, or

   ✓ that the patented invention is not worked in the territory of India.

b) Where the Controller directs the patentee to grant a license he may as incidental thereto exercise the powers set out in section – 88 of the Indian Patent Act.

c) If the patented invention is needed in times of national emergency or other circumstances of extreme urgency or in the case of public non-commercial use or on establishment of a ground of anti-competitive practices adopted by the patentee.

d) The demand for the patented article has not been met to an adequate extent or on reasonable terms,

e) The establishment or development of commercial activities in India is prejudiced, etc.

The Compulsory License may be terminated according to Section – 94 of the Indian Patents Act.

- on an application made by the patentee or any other person deriving title or interest in the patent, a compulsory license granted under Section – 84 may be terminated by the Controller, if and when the circumstances that gave rise to the grant thereof no longer exist and such circumstances are unlikely to recur. Provided that the holder of the compulsory license shall have the right to object such termination; and

- while considering an application under sub-section (1), the Controller shall take into account that the interest of the person who had previously been granted the license is not unduly prejudiced.

Nature of Information needed while consulting a Patent Attorney/Agent:

As an inventor one should share the complete invention details with a patent attorney in the same manner as a patient confides in a doctor. A Patent Attorney is able to draft a good specification only if the inventor provides the complete details of the invention. The following points should be kept in mind while discussing with the Patent Attorney, since patent specification is a techno-legal document:

- Provide complete details of the invention including failures, if any, on the way to the invention. Do not feel hesitant and bad to answer any of the questions raised by the patent attorney. The inventor may even need to show the laboratory, note books, log books, etc., if necessary.

- Explain the central theme of the invention and novelty, inventiveness and utility of the invention.

- Share all the prior-art documents in your possession with the attorney.

- If you have developed an improved version of your competitor's product/process, admit it and be totally honest. This would help the attorney in drafting precise claims and avoid excessive claims, which might be struck down immediately or at a later date.

- A detailed description of the best way of putting the invention into practical use, results of your tests and trials, etc., including all failures and defects should be given to an attorney.

- Alternative ways of using the invention, and the substitutes or parts of it.

- It may e worth drafting the patent widely enough to cover less satisfactory alternatives as well so as to prevent rivals from marketing a less satisfactory competing product, which because of its defects might bring the whole genre of product into disrepute or which may be cheap.

- Both after an initial search and during the course of the filing and grant of a patent application, it is important to respond quickly and accurately to queries that the Patent attorney may have. Thus, the client should keep the Patent Attorney informed of any new developments in the field of invention carried by the patentee or someone else.

Patent infringement:

The law does not define infringement. However, violation of any rights of the patentee by an unauthorized third party would consider infringement. Thus, any action that interferes with the full enjoyment of the monopoly granted to the patentee is an infringement, if done without his consent.

Generally, infringement is committed where any person without license from the patentee either directly or indirectly makes uses or puts into practice the invention that is embraced by claims. In other word, direct infringement is one where there is direct taking of the element of the patented invention. The indirect infringement is where the element of the patented invention is not taken as such. The alleged infringing device will be achieved by inventing around the patented one. The elements of the patented invention will be couched by some significant alteration so as to make it appear as new one.

The infringement of a patent can be done in a number of ways, one of which is by using the patent or any colorable imitation in the manufacture of patented article. The infringement need not be of the whole of the process but it may be only a part of it. In the case of a patent of a combination, the patent is for that particular combination only. None of them dealt separately will be protected by the patent monopoly. If one part is replaced without affecting the whole or substantial part of the invention, there is no infringement. It is deemed only as a repair and not as inventing something new.

The Patents (Amendment) Act, 2002 inserted new Section – 107A dealing with certain acts not to be considered as infringement. This new section makes the following act not to be considered as infringement of patent rights.

a) Any act of making, constructing, using or selling a patented invention solely for uses reasonably related to the development and submission of information required under any law for the time being in force, in India, or in a country other than India, that regulates the manufacture, construction, use or sale of any product.

b) Importation of patented products by any person from a person who is duly authorized by the patentee to sell or distribute the product.

Relief in Suits for Infringement:

According to Section – 108 of Indian Patent Act, 2002,

- the relief which a court may grant in any suit for infringement includes an injunction (subject to such terms, if any, as the court thinks fit and, at the option of the plaintiff, either damages or an account of profits).

- the court may also order that the goods which are found to be infringing and materials and implement, the predominant use of which is in the creation of infringing goods shall be seized, forfeited or destroyed, as the court deems fit under the circumstances of the case without payment of any compensation.

Relief under TRIPS agreement:

The patentee is entitled to get the following relief in case of successfully infringement proceedings:

a) injunction (Article - 44)

b) damages (Article - 45)

c) other remedies (Article - 46)

d) right to information (Article – 47)

e) indemnification of the defendant (Article – 48)

If the patentee believes that others are infringing his or her patent, then, the first step, the patentee need to collect information about infringing parties and their use of the infringing product or process. The patentee should accumulate all available facts to determine the nature and timing of his action. The patentee has always engage a patent lawyer to assist him in making a decision on the infringement of his patented invention. In some cases, when infringement id detected, companies choose to send a letter (commonly known a s a '**cease and desist letter**') informing the alleged infringer of a possible conflict between of the patentee's rights and the other company's business activity. This procedure is often effective in the case of non-intentional infringement since the infringer will in many such cases either discontinue such activities or agree to negotiate a **licensing agreement**.

Sometimes, however, surprise is the best tactic in order to avoid giving the infringer time to hide or destroy evidence. In these circumstances, it might be appropriate to go to court without giving notice to the infringer and to ask for an '**interim injunction**' in order to surprise the infringer by a raid, often with the help of the police, at his business premises. The court may order that the alleged infringers stop their infringing action pending the outcome of a trial (which may take many months or years). However, the question of whether a patent has been infringed may be very complex and a decision may, therefore, only be taken in proceedings on the merits of the case.

Where the company decides to initiate **civil proceedings**, the courts generally provide a wide range of civil remedies to compensate aggrieved owners of patent rights. A patent lawyer will be able to provide the patentee the relevant information.

In order to prevent the information of goods infringing patents, measures at the international border may be available to patent holder in some countries through the national customs authorities. Many countries, however, provide for better measures in accordance with their international obligation only in cases of importation of counterfeit trademark goods and pirated copyright goods.

As a general rule, if the patentee identifies the infringement of his or her patent rights, it is highly advisable to seek professional legal advice.

Alternative dispute resolution:

- (what are the options of the patentee for settling the patent infringement out of court?)

If the dispute is with a company with which there is a signed contract (e.g., a licensing agreement), then first check whether there is an **arbitration or mediation** clause in the contract. It is advisable to include a special provision in contracts for the dispute to be referred to arbitration or mediation in order to avoid long and expensive litigation. It may be possible to use alternative dispute resolution systems, such as arbitration of mediation, even if there is no clause in the contract or no contract at all, as long as both parties agree to it.

Arbitration generally has the advantage of being a less formal and shorter procedure than court proceedings, and an arbitral award is more easily enforceable internationally. An advantage or mediation is that the parties retain control of the dispute resolution process. As such, it can help to preserve good business relations with another enterprise with which the patentee company may with to collaborate in the future. The **WIPO Arbitration and Mediation Centre** provides services for alternative dispute resolution.

Agreements and Treaties   4

4.1: General Agreement on Trade and Tariff (GATT)

The **General Agreement on Tariffs and Trade (GATT)** was negotiated during the UN Conference on Trade and Employment and was the outcome of the failure of negotiating governments to create the *International Trade Organization* (ITO). GATT was signed in 1947 and lasted until 1993, when it was replaced by the **World Trade Organization** in 1995. The original GATT text (GATT 1947) is still in effect under the WTO framework, subject to the modifications of GATT 1994. the General Agreement on Tariffs and Trade (GATT), was established after World War II in the wake of other new multilateral institutions dedicated to international economic cooperation notably the ***Bretton Woods institutions*** known as the ***World Bank*** and ***the International Monetary Fund.*** A comparable international institution for trade, named the ***International Trade Organization*** was successfully negotiated. The ITO was to be a United Nations specialized agency and would address not only trade barriers but other issues indirectly related to trade, including employment, investment, restrictive business practices, and commodity agreements. But the ITO treaty was not approved by the U.S. and a few other signatories and never went into effect.

The **General Agreement on Tariffs and Trade** (GATT) is a multilateral agreement regulating trade among 153 countries. According to its preamble, the purpose of the GATT is the "substantial reduction of tariffs and other trade barriers and the elimination of preferences, on a reciprocal and mutually advantageous basis."

The GATT functioned *de facto* as an organization, conducting **eight rounds** of talks addressing various trade issues and resolving international trade disputes.

GATT and WTO trade rounds					
Name	Start	Duration	Countries	Subjects covered	Achievements
Geneva	April 1947	7 months	23	Tariffs	Signing of GATT, 45,000 tariff concessions affecting $10 billion of trade
Annecy	April 1949	5 months	13	Tariffs	Countries exchanged some 5,000 tariff concessions
Torquay	September 1950	8 months	38	Tariffs	Countries exchanged some 8,700 tariff concessions, cutting the 1948 tariff levels by 25%

(Contd.)

GATT and WTO trade rounds					
Name	**Start**	**Duration**	**Countries**	**Subjects covered**	**Achievements**
Geneva II	January 1956	5 months	26	Tariffs, admission of Japan	$2.5 billion in tariff reductions
Dillon	September 1960	11 months	26	Tariffs	Tariff concessions worth $4.9 billion of world trade
Kennedy	May 1964	37 months	62	Tariffs, Anti-dumping	Tariff concessions worth $40 billion of world trade
Tokyo	September 1973	74 months	102	Tariffs, non-tariff measures, "framework" agreements	Tariff reductions worth more than $300 billion dollars achieved
Uruguay	September 1986	87 months	123	Tariffs, non-tariff measures, rules, services, intellectual property, dispute settlement, textiles, agriculture, creation of WTO, etc	The round led to the creation of WTO, and extended the range of trade negotiations, leading to major reductions in tariffs (about 40%) and agricultural subsidies, an agreement to allow full access for textiles and clothing from developing countries, and an extension of intellectual property rights.
Doha	November 2001	NA	141	Tariffs, non-tariff measures, agriculture, labor standards, environment, competition, investment, transparency, patents etc	The round is not yet concluded.

Annecy Round – 1949: The second round took place in 1949 in Annecy, France. 33 countries took part in the round. The main focus of the talks was more tariff reductions, around 5000 in total.

Torquay Round – 1951: The third round occurred in Torquay, England in 1950. Thirty-eight countries took part in the round. 8,700 tariff concessions were made totaling the remaining amount of tariffs to ¾ of the tariffs which were in effect in 1948. The contemporaneous rejection by the U.S. of the Havana Charter signified the establishment of the GATT as a governing world body.

Geneva Round - 1955–1956: The fourth round returned to Geneva in 1955 and lasted until May 1956. Twenty-six countries took part in the round. $2.5 billion in tariffs were eliminated or reduced.

Dillon Round - 1960–1962: The fifth round occurred once more in Geneva and lasted from 1960–1962. The talks were named after U.S. Treasury Secretary and former Under Secretary of State, Douglas Dillon, who first proposed the talks. Twenty-six countries took part in the round. Along with reducing over $4.9 billion in tariffs, it also yielded discussion relating to the creation of the European Economic Community (EEC).

Kennedy Round - 1964–1967: Kennedy Round took place from 1964–1967. $40 billion in tariffs were eliminated or reduced.

Tokyo Round - 1973–1979: Reduced tariffs and established new regulations aimed at controlling the proliferation of non-tariff barriers and voluntary export restrictions. 102 countries took part in the round. Concessions were made on $190 billion worth.

Uruguay Round - 1986–1994: The Uruguay Round began in 1986. It was the most ambitious round to date, hoping to expand the competence of the GATT to important new areas such as services, capital, intellectual property, textiles, and agriculture. 123 countries took part in the round. The Uruguay Round was also the first set of multilateral trade negotiations in which developing countries had played an active role.

Agriculture was essentially exempted from previous agreements as it was given special status in the areas of import quotas and export subsidies, with only mild caveats. However, by the time of the Uruguay round, many countries considered the exception of agriculture to be sufficiently glaring that they refused to sign a new deal without some movement on agricultural products. These fourteen countries came to be known as the "*Cairns Group*," and included mostly small and medium sized agricultural exporters such as Australia, Brazil, Canada, Indonesia, and New Zealand.

The Agreement on Agriculture of the Uruguay Round continues to be the most substantial trade liberalization agreement in agricultural products in the history of trade negotiations. The goals of the agreement were to improve market access for agricultural products, reduce domestic support of agriculture in the form of price-distorting subsidies and quotas, eliminate over time export subsidies on agricultural products and to harmonize to the extent possible sanitary and phytosanitary measures between member countries.

The Uruguay Round, which was completed on December 15, 1993 after seven years of negotiations, resulted in an agreement among 117 countries (including the U.S.) to reduce trade barriers and to create more comprehensive and enforceable world trade rules. The agreement coming out of this round, the Final Act Embodying the Results of the Uruguay Round of Multilateral Trade Negotiations, was signed in April 1994. The Uruguay Round agreement was approved and implemented by the U.S. Congress in December 1994, and went into effect on January 1, 1995. This agreement also created the **World Trade Organization** (WTO), which came into being on January 1, 1995. The WTO implements the agreement, provides a forum for negotiating additional reductions of trade barriers and for settling policy disputes, and enforces trade rules. The WTO launched the ninth round of multilateral trade negotiations under the "Doha Development Agenda" (DDA or Doha Round) in 2001.

4.2: Trade Related Aspects of Intellectual Property Rights (TRIPS)

The Agreement on Trade Related Aspects of Intellectual Property Rights (TRIPS) is an international agreement administered by the World Trade Organization (WTO) that sets down minimum standards for many forms of intellectual property (IP) regulation as applied to nationals of the WTO Members.. It was negotiated at the end of the Uruguay Round of the General Agreement on Tariffs and Trade (GATT) in 1994 (i.e., the TRIPS Agreement is Annex 1C of the Marrakesh Agreement Establishing the World Trade Organization, signed in Marrakesh, Morocco on 15 April 1994) which came into effect on 1st January 1995. The TRIPS agreement introduced intellectual property law into the international trading system for the first time and remains the most comprehensive international agreement on intellectual property to date.

TRIPS contains requirements that nations' laws must meet for copyright rights, including the rights of performers, producers of sound recordings and broadcasting organizations; geographical indications, including appellations of origin; industrial designs; integrated circuit layout-designs; patents; monopolies for the developers of new plant varieties; trademarks; trade dress; and undisclosed or confidential information. TRIPS also specifies enforcement procedures, remedies, and dispute resolution procedures.

As per the TRIPS the protection and enforcement of all intellectual property rights shall meet the objectives to contribute to the promotion of technological innovation and to the transfer and dissemination of technology, to the mutual advantage of producers and users of technological knowledge and in a manner conducive to social and economic welfare, and to a balance of rights and obligations. In 2001, developing countries, concerned that developed countries were insisting on an overly narrow reading of TRIPS, initiated a round of talks that resulted in the Doha Declaration. The Doha declaration is a WTO statement that clarifies the scope of TRIPS, stating for example that TRIPS can and should be interpreted in light of the goal "to promote access to medicines for all."

Historical Overview of TRIPS:

TRIPS was negotiated at the end of the Uruguay Round of the General Agreement on Tariffs and Trade (GATT) in 1994. Its inclusion was the culmination of a program of intense lobbying by the United States, supported by the European Union, Japan and other developed nations. Campaigns of unilateral economic encouragement under the Generalized System of Preferences and coercion under Section 301 of the Trade Act played an important role in defeating competing policy positions that were favored by developing countries, most notably Korea and Brazil, but also including Thailand, India and Caribbean Basin states. In turn, the United States strategy of linking trade policy to intellectual property standards can be traced back to the entrepreneurship of senior management at Pfizer in the early 1980s, who mobilized corporations in the United States and made maximizing intellectual property privileges the number one priority of trade policy in the United States.

After the Uruguay round, the GATT became the basis for the establishment of the World Trade Organization. Because ratification of TRIPS is a compulsory requirement of World Trade Organization membership, any country seeking to obtain easy access to the numerous international markets opened by the World Trade Organization must enact the strict intellectual property laws mandated by TRIPS. For this reason, TRIPS is the most important multilateral instrument for the globalization of intellectual property laws. States like Russia and China that were very unlikely to join the Berne Convention have found the prospect of WTO membership a powerful enticement.

Furthermore, unlike other agreements on intellectual property, TRIPS has a powerful enforcement mechanism. States can be disciplined through the WTO's dispute settlement mechanism.

Features of the TRIPS agreement:

1. **Standards**. In respect of each of the main areas of intellectual property covered by the TRIPS Agreement, the Agreement sets out the minimum standards of protection to be provided by each Member. Each of the

main elements of protection is defined, namely the subject-matter to be protected, the rights to be conferred and permissible exceptions to those rights, and the minimum duration of protection. The Agreement sets these standards by requiring, first, that the substantive obligations of the main conventions of the WIPO, the Paris Convention for the Protection of Industrial Property (Paris Convention) and the Berne Convention for the Protection of Literary and Artistic Works (Berne Convention) in their most recent versions must be complied with.

2. **Enforcement**. The second main set of provisions deals with domestic procedures and remedies for the enforcement of intellectual property rights. The Agreement lays down certain general principles applicable to all IPR enforcement procedures. In addition, it contains provisions on civil and administrative procedures and remedies, provisional measures, special requirements related to border measures and criminal procedures, which specify, in a certain amount of detail, the procedures and remedies that must be available so that right holders can effectively enforce their rights.

3. **Dispute settlement**. The Agreement makes disputes between WTO Members in respect of TRIPS obligations subject to the WTO's dispute settlement procedures.

The requirements of TRIPS:

TRIPS requires member nations to provide strong protection for intellectual property rights. The basic requirements of as under TRIPS:

- Copyright terms must extend to 50 years after the death of the author; although films and photographs are only required to habve fixed 50 and 25 years respectively.

- Copyright must be granted automatically, and not based upon any "formality," such as registrations or systems of renewal.

- Computer programs must be regarded as "literary works" under copyright law and receive the same terms of protection.

- National exceptions to copyright (such as "fair use" in the United States) are constrained.

- Patents must be granted in all "fields of technology," although exceptions for certain public interests are allowed and must be enforceable for at least 20 years.

- Exceptions to exclusive rights must be limited, provided that a normal exploitation of the work (Art. 13) and normal exploitation of the patent (Art 30) is not in conflict.

- No unreasonable prejudice to the legitimate interests of the right holders of computer programs and patents is allowed.

- Legitimate interests of third parties have to be taken into account by patent rights (Art 30).

- In each nation, intellectual property laws may not offer any benefits to local citizens which are not available to citizens of other TRIPS signatories under the principle of national treatment. TRIPS also has a most favored nation (MFN)clause.

Many of the TRIPS provisions on copyright were copied from the Berne Convention for the Protection of Literary and Artistic Works and many of its trademark and patent provisions were modeled on the Paris Convention for the Protection of Industrial Property.

Implementation of TRIPS in developing countries:

The obligations under TRIPS apply equally to all member states, however developing countries were allowed extra time to implement the applicable changes to their national laws, in two tiers of transition according to their level of development. The transition period for developing countries expired in 2005. The transition period for least developed countries to implement TRIPS was extended to 2013, and until 1 January 2016 for pharmaceutical patents, with the possibility of further extension.

It has therefore been argued that the TRIPS standard of requiring all countries to create strict intellectual property systems will be detrimental to poorer countries' development.Many argue that it is, *prima facie*, in the strategic interest of most if not all underdeveloped nations to use any flexibility available in TRIPS to legislate the weakest IP laws possible.

This has not happened in most cases. A 2005 report by the WHO found that many developing countries have not incorporated TRIPS flexibilities (compulsory licensing, parallel importation, limits on data protection, use of broad research and other exceptions to patentability, etc.) into their legislation to the extent authorized under Doha.

This is likely caused by the lack of legal and technical expertise needed to draft legislation that implements flexibilities, which has often led to developing countries directly copying developed country IP legislation, or relying on technical assistance from the World Intellectual Property Organization (WIPO), which, according to the critics encourages them to implement stronger intellectual property monopolies.

Post-TRIPS expansion:

The requirements of TRIPS are, from a policy perspective, extremely stringent. Despite this, lobbyists for the industries that benefit from various intellectual property laws have continued since 1994 to campaign to strengthen existing forms of intellectual property and to create new kinds:

- The creation of anti-circumvention laws to protect Digital Rights Management systems. This was achieved through the 1996 World Intellectual Property Organization Copyright Treaty (WIPO Treaty) and the WIPO Performances and Phonograms Treaty.

- The desire to further restrict the possibility of compulsory licenses for patents has led to provisions in recent bilateral US trade agreements.

- It is one thing for states to have intellectual property laws on their statutes, and another for governments to enforce them aggressively. This distinction has led to provisions in bilateral agreements, as well as proposals for WIPO and European Union rules on intellectual property enforcement. The 2001 EU Copyright Directive was to implement the 1996 WIPO Copyright Treaty.

- The wording of TRIPS Art 27 of non-discrimination is used to justify an extension of the patent system.

- The campaign for the creation of a WIPO Broadcasting Treaty that would give broadcasters (and possibly webcasters) exclusive rights over the copies of works they have distributed.

Protection of Computer Programs and Compilation of Data:

As per Berne Convention Copyright protection shall extend to expressions and not to ideas, procedures, methods of operation or mathematical concepts as such.

- The Computer programs, whether in source or object code, shall be protected as literary works under the Berne Convention (1971)

- Compilations of data or other material, whether in machine readable or other form, which by reason of the selection or arrangement of their contents constitute intellectual creations shall be protected as such. Such protection, which shall not extend to the data or material itself, shall be without prejudice to any copyright subsisting in the data or material itself.

In respect of at least computer programs and cinematographic works, a Member shall provide authors and their successors in title the right to authorize or to prohibit the commercial rental to the public of originals or copies of their copyright works. A Member shall be exempted from this obligation in respect of cinematographic works unless such rental has led to widespread copying of such works which is materially impairing the exclusive right of reproduction conferred in that Member on authors and their successors in title. In respect of computer programs, this obligation does not apply to rentals where the program itself is not the essential object of the rental.

Whenever the term of protection of a work, other than a photographic work or a work of applied art, is calculated on a basis other than the life of a natural person, such term shall be no less than 50 years from the end of the calendar year of authorized publication, or, failing such authorized publication within 50 years from the making of the work, 50 years from the end of the calendar year of making.

Council for Trade-Related Aspects of Intellectual Property Rights:

The Council for TRIPS shall monitor the operation of this Agreement and, in particular, Members' compliance with their obligations hereunder, and shall afford Members the opportunity of consulting on matters relating to the trade-related aspects of intellectual property rights. It shall carry out such other responsibilities as assigned to it by the Members, and it shall, in particular, provide any assistance requested by them in the context of dispute settlement procedures. In carrying out its functions, the Council for TRIPS may consult with and seek information from any source it deems appropriate. In consultation with WIPO, the Council shall seek to establish, within one year of its first meeting, appropriate arrangements for cooperation with bodies of that Organization.

The role of the TRIPS Council:

The TRIPS Council comprises all WTO members. It is responsible for monitoring the operation of the agreement, and, in particular, how members comply with their obligations under it.

1. Monitoring - Members review each others' laws:

The reviews are central to the TRIPS Council's task of monitoring what is happening under the agreement.

Each country has to make sure its laws comply with the obligations of the agreement, according to the timetable spelt out in the agreement. Most have to enact laws implementing the obligations.

These laws are notified to the TRIPS Council, allowing members to review each others' legislation, and promoting the transparency of members' policies on intellectual property protection.

The requirement to notify comes under Article 63.2 of the TRIPS Agreement. Members have to supply the TRIPS Council with copies of their laws and regulations that deal with the TRIPS Agreements' provisions.

These notifications are then used as the basis the Council's reviews of members' legislation. In these reviews, countries supply written questions about each others' laws before the review meetings. The answers are also in writing. Follow-up questions and replies are made orally during the course of the meeting, and further follow-up is possible at subsequent meetings.

2. Consultations - On any TRIPS issue:

The TRIPS Council is also a forum that countries can use to consult each other on problems they may have with each other to do with the TRIPS Agreement. It can also clarify or interpret provisions of the agreement.

3. Technical Cooperation - A work programme:

The Council follows a work programme on technical cooperation with a view to monitoring how developed countries fulfill their obligations under Article 67 of the TRIPS Agreement.

This article sets out the developed countries' commitments on technical cooperation. The work programme ensures that developing countries can have adequate information on the assistance on offer. It also ensures any of their unfulfilled needs are identified and responded to.

4. Reviews and Negotiations on Specific Subjects:

The WTO is a forum for further negotiations aimed at enhanced commitments in the area of intellectual property, as in other areas covered by the WTO agreements.

The TRIPS Agreement calls for further work in specified areas, including:

- the negotiation of a multilateral system of notification and registration for geographical indications for wines (Article 23.4);

- the review of the application of provisions on protecting geographical indications (Article 24.2);

- the review, after four years, of the option to exclude from patentability certain plant and animal inventions (Article 27.3(b));

- and the examination of the applicability to TRIPS of non-violation complaints under the dispute settlement process (Article 64).

5. Review of TRIPS Agreement:

The TRIPS Council will hold a general review of the agreement after five years; but it is also empowered to review it at any time in the light of any relevant new developments which might warrant modification and amendment (Article 71).

Does the TRIPS Agreement apply to all WTO members?

All the WTO agreements (except for a couple of "plurilateral" agreements) apply to all WTO members. The members each accepted all the agreements as a single package with a single signature — making it, in the jargon, a "single undertaking."

The TRIPS Agreement is part of that package. Therefore it applies to all WTO members. (More on the single undertaking.) However, the agreement allows countries different periods of time to delay applying its provisions. These delays define the transition from before the agreement came into force (before 1 January 1995) until it is applied in member countries. The main transition periods are:

- Developed countries were granted a transition period of one year following the entry into force of the WTO Agreement, i.e. until 1 January 1996.

- Developing countries were allowed a further period of four years (i.e. to 1 January 2000) to apply the provisions of the agreement other than Articles 3, 4 and 5 which deal with general principles such as non-discrimination.

- Transition economies, i.e. members in the process of transformation from centrally-planned into market economies, could also benefit from the same delay (also until 1 January 2000) if they met certain additional conditions.

Least-developed countries are granted a longer transition period of a total of eleven years (until 1 January 2006), with the possibility of an extension. For pharmaceutical patents, this has been extended to

1 January 2016, under a decision taken by ministers All members, even those availing themselves of the longer transitional periods, have had to comply with obligations on national treatment (equal treatment for foreign and domestic individuals and companies, Article 3) and most-favoured-nation treatment (non-discrimination between foreign individuals and companies, Article 4) from 1 January 1996.

The TRIPS Agreement requires members to comply with certain minimum standards for the protection of intellectual property rights covered in it. But Members may choose to implement laws which give more extensive protection than is required in the agreement, so long as the additional protection does not contravene the provisions of the agreement. This is why the TRIPS Agreement is sometimes described as a "minimum standards" agreement.

In addition, the agreement gives members the freedom to determine the appropriate method of implementing the provisions of the agreement within their own legal system and practice. The agreement thus takes into account the diversity of members' legal frameworks (for instance between common law and civil law traditions).

Controversy and Criticism:

Since TRIPS came into force it has received a growing level of criticism from developing countries, academics, and Non-governmental organizations. Some of this criticism is against the WTO as a whole, but many advocates of trade liberalization also regard TRIPS as bad policy. TRIPS' wealth redistribution effects (moving money from people in developing countries to copyright and patent owners in developed countries) and its imposition of artificial scarcity on the citizens of countries that would otherwise have had weaker intellectual property laws, are a common basis for such criticisms.

Another controversy has been over the TRIPS Article 27 requirements for patentability "in all fields of technology," and whether or not this necessitates the granting of software and business method patents.

4.3: World Trade Organization

In 1993, the GATT was updated (*GATT 1994*) to include new obligations upon its signatories. One of the most significant changes was the creation of the World Trade Organization (WTO). The **World Trade Organization (WTO)** is an organization that intends to supervise and liberalize international trade. The organization officially commenced on January 1, 1995 under the *Marrakech Agreement*, replacing the General Agreement on Tariffs and Trade (GATT), which commenced in 1948. There are a total of 157 member countries and 26 observers in the WTO.

The GATT was a set of rules agreed upon by nations, whereas the WTO is an institutional body. The organization deals with regulation of trade between participating countries; it provides a framework for negotiating and formalizing trade agreements, and a dispute resolution process aimed at enforcing participants' adherence to WTO agreements which are signed by representatives of member governments and ratified by their parliaments. *There are a number of ways of looking at the World Trade Organization. It is an organization for trade opening. It is a forum for governments to negotiate trade agreements. It is a place for them to settle trade disputes. It operates a system of trade rules. Essentially, the WTO is a place where member governments try to sort out the trade problems they face with each other.*

Objectives of WTO:

The World Trade Organization (WTO) deals with the global rules of trade between nations. Its main Objectives are

- to ensure that trade flows as smoothly, predictably and freely as possible

- to expand world production and trade,

- optimal utilization of world's resources; and

- to raise the living standards and the income of the people of the world.

The principles and functions of the WTO aim to protect and promote the interests of the developing countries by providing more time to adjust, greater flexibility and special privileges. The WTO provides a forum for continuous negotiations among the members, which include the efforts for further liberalization of trade in goods and services and also for developing discipline in other trade related areas. The WTO further provides procedures and rules to settle trade disputes among members when infringements occur.

WTO and Trade Agreements:

Most of the issues that the WTO focuses on derive from previous trade negotiations, especially from the Uruguay Round (1986–1994) The WTO expanded its scope from traded goods to trade within the service sector and intellectual property rights. Although it was designed to serve multilateral agreements, during several rounds of GATT negotiations (particularly the Tokyo Round) plurilateral agreements created selective trading and caused fragmentation among members. WTO arrangements are generally a multilateral agreement settlement mechanism of GATT. The agreements fall into a structure with six main parts:

- The Agreement Establishing the WTO

- Goods and investment — the Multilateral Agreements on Trade in Goods including the GATT 1994 and the Trade Related Investment Measures

- Services — the General Agreement on Trade in Services (GATS)

- Intellectual property — the Agreement on Trade-Related Aspects of Intellectual Property Rights (TRIPS)

- Dispute settlement (DSU)

- Reviews of governments' trade policies (TPRM)

There are elaborate agreements on 12 subjects in the area of trade in good, viz.,

- Agriculture

- Textiles and Clothing

- Trade Related Investment Measures (TRIMs)

- Sanitary and Phyto-sanitary Measures (SPS)

- Technical Barriers to Trade (TBT)

- Anti-Dumping

- Customs Valuation

- Pre-shipment Inspection

- Rules of Origin

- Import Licensing

- Subsidies and Countervailing Measures

- Safeguards.

Administration of WTO:

The WTO is run by its member governments. All major decisions are made by the membership as a whole, either by ministers (who usually meet at least once every two years, i.e., the ministerial conference) or by their ambassadors or delegates (who meet regularly in Geneva).

The WTO is governed by its topmost decision-making body *Ministerial Conference*, meeting every two years; a General Council (the general council as an important body of WTO has two subsidiary bodies – 'the Dispute Settlement body' and 'the Trade Policy Review body'), which implements the conference's policy decisions and is responsible for day-to-day administration; and a director-general, who is appointed by the ministerial conference. The Ministerial Conference brings together all members of the WTO, all of which are countries or customs unions. The Ministerial Conference can take decisions on all matters under any of the multilateral trade agreements. The WTO's headquarters is at the *Centre William Rappard, Geneva, Switzerland.*

The General Council of WTO has multiple bodies which oversee committees in different areas are the following:

1. Council for Trade in Goods

There are 11 committees under the jurisdiction of the Goods Council each with a specific task. All members of the WTO participate in the committees. The Textiles Monitoring Body is separate from the other committees but still under the jurisdiction of Goods Council. The body has its own chairman and only 10 members. The body also has several groups relating to textiles.

2. Council for Trade-Related Aspects of Intellectual Property Rights

Information on intellectual property in the WTO, news and official records of the activities of the TRIPS Council, and details of the WTO's work with other international organizations in the field.

3. Council for Trade in Services

The Council for Trade in Services operates under the guidance of the General Council and is responsible for overseeing the functioning of the General Agreement on Trade in Services (GATS). It is open to all WTO members, and can create subsidiary bodies as required. The Council for Trade in Services has three subsidiary bodies: financial services, domestic regulations, GATS rules and specific commitments.

4. Trade Negotiations Committee

The Trade Negotiations Committee (TNC) is the committee that deals with the current trade talks round. The chair is WTO's director-general. The committee is currently tasked with the Doha Development Round.

The General council has several different committees, working groups, and working parties. There are committees on the following: Trade and Environment; Trade and Development (Subcommittee on Least-Developed Countries); Regional Trade Agreements; Balance of Payments Restrictions; and Budget, Finance and Administration. There are working parties on the following: Accession. There are working groups on the following: Trade, debt and finance; and Trade and technology transfer.

While the WTO is driven by its member states, it could not function without its Secretariat to coordinate the activities. The Secretariat employs over 600 staff, and its experts — lawyers, economists, statisticians and communications experts — assist WTO members on a daily basis to ensure, among other things, that negotiations progress smoothly, and that the rules of international trade are correctly applied and enforced.

Settlement of Disputes:

In 1994, the WTO members agreed on the Understanding on Rules and Procedures Governing the Settlement of Disputes (DSU) annexed to the "Final Act" signed in Marrakesh in 1994. Dispute settlement is regarded by the WTO as the central pillar of the multilateral trading system, and as a *unique contribution to the stability and predictability of the global economy.*" WTO members have agreed that, if they believe fellow-members are violating trade rules, they will use the multilateral system of settling disputes instead of taking action unilaterally.

The operation of the WTO dispute settlement process involves the DSB panels, the Appellate Body, the WTO Secretariat, arbitrators, independent experts and several specialized institutions. Bodies involved in the dispute settlement process, World Trade Organization.   The dispute settlement forum of the WTO is one forum where stranger partnerships. India and Pakistan united against the USA, the US agains EU, US against Canada, tiny Banana Republics against major powers, developing versus the developed, developing versus the developing. The comment that there are no permanent friends, only permanent interests that appears accurate in relation with respect to International Trade.

The working of the DSU has no doubt created an efficient forum for countries to resolve their differences, it permits countries to pursue their rights independent of considerations of economic power, but its working in a way seems to have resulted in the countries having got more than they has asked for. Sovereignty has been the touchiest issue, which the DSU has been charged to have undermined. The debate as to how much difference the panel and the Appllate Body must show to national interest or aspirations of domestic constituency or even decisions of national courts remains a matter of controversy. Many countries seem to be unhappy that they have perforce to get their legislations and policies modified in line with WTO rulings. There is also vehement criticism that dispute settlement under the GATT seems to give an overriding importance to free trade trumping legitimate interest such as enviornment, biodiversity, culture and balance of payment.

Dispute Settlement Mechanism:

The Dispute Settlement Mechanism under the WTO is the subject matter of Chapter 27 under Section V and it works as follows. At first, when one country believes that another is violating any aspect of the agreement (including GATS, TRIPS and also GATT), the compalining country first requests consultation with the offending country, and the two seek to resolve the dispute on their own. If consultation fails, then the complaining country requests establishment of a panel, consisting of three persons with appropriate expertise form countries not party to the dispute. This panel assesses the evidence in the context of its interpretation of the WTO members, acting through their Dispute Settlement Body (DSB), decide by conensus against its adoption, or if one of the parties to the dispute voices its intention to appeal. Therefore, the process requires unanimity among WTO members not to accept a panel report, in marked contrast to the procedures of the old GATT, where a panel report could be blocked by any one country, including the country that was complained for.

To hear appeals, the WTO has established an Appllate Body, composed of seven memnbers of which three will serve on any given case. This Appellate Body is to consider only issues of law and legal interpretations by the panel, and it too issues a report which must be accepted by a unanimous decision of the DSB.

Once this process is completed, countries are expectedc to implement any recommendations of the panel report. If they do not, then complaining countries are entitled to compensation from them, or to use suspension of concessions (usually increased trade barriers) against them.

Following are some of the examples to quote the international trade disputes settled by the WTO intervention:

- Trutle – Shrimp Case
- Canadian Periodicals case
- Japan – Taxes on Alcoholic Beverages and Chile – Taxes on Alcoholic Beverages
- Thai Cigarette Case, etc.

Anti – Dumping Measures:

In international trade, 'dumping' occurs when an exporting country (exporter) 'dumps' or sells goods in the importing country at price lower than their costs in the exporting country. The provisions with respect to anti-dumping measures:

- According to GATT, 1994, member nations have a right to impose anti-dumping measures under two conditions:
  - ✓ a product is supplied at an export price which is below 'normal' value, i.e., a price which is lower than the domestic cost in the exporting country; and
  - ✓ the 'dumped' imports are shown to cause serious damage to a domestic industry located in the importing country.
- Rules for determining 'dumping' are provided by GATT. Criteria are provided for allocating costs for determining normal value and for determining the causal relation between 'dumped' imports and injury to a domestic industry.
- Procedures are set out in detail to deal with anti-dumping cases.
- Anti-dumping measures should expire after five years.
- Anti-dumping measures are not allowed to be applied when the price of 'dumped' imports is lower by 2% or less of the normal value or when the quantity of imports dumped is negligible., i.e., 3% or less of total imports of the product imported by a country.

Environmental Aspects of International Trade:

The WTO has been under intense pressure to legitimize the use of trade measures for environmental purposes as they are percived as effective tools for ensuring compliance with environmental standards. However, the WTO may not be an appropriate forum to deal with global environmental issues.

From the trade perspective, environment issues can be divided into trading in commodities that affect the environment of:

- Importing country
- Exporting country
- Global (or trade-boundary) environment.

Functions of WTO:

Among the various functions of the WTO, these are regarded by analysts as the most important:

- It oversees the implementation, administration and operation of the covered agreements,
- To supervise on a regular basis the operations of the revised GATT agreements and ministerial declarations,

- It provides a forum for negotiations and for settling disputes (i.e., to act as a Dispute Settlement Body),

- Serving as a Trade Review mechanism,

- Assisting developing countries with trade policy issues through technical assistance and training programme,

- To establish various councils such as the goods council, services council, TRIPS council as subsidiary bodies, etc.

Additionally, it is the WTO's duty to review and propagate the national trade policies, and to ensure the coherence and transparency of trade policies through surveillance in global economic policy-making. Another priority of the WTO is the assistance of developing, least-developed and low-income countries in transition to adjust to WTO rules and disciplines through technical cooperation and training.

The WTO is also a center of economic research and analysis - regular assessments of the global trade picture in its annual publications and research reports on specific topics are produced by the organization. Finally, the WTO cooperates closely with the two other components of the Bretton Woods system - the IMF and the World Bank.

Since 1995, WTO has become the engine as well as the vehicle to promote globalization in all spheres of economic life of the member nations world wide.

WTO Principles of Trade Policy:

The WTO establishes a framework for trade policies; it does not define or specify outcomes. That is, it is concerned with setting the rules of the trade policy games. Five principles are of particular importance in understanding both the pre-1994 GATT and the WTO:

1. **Non-Discrimination**: It has two major components: the most favoured nation (MFN) rule, and the national treatment policy. Both are embedded in the main WTO rules on goods, services, and intellectual property, but their precise scope and nature differ across these areas. The MFN rule requires that a WTO member must apply the same conditions on all trade with other WTO members, i.e. a WTO member has to grant the most favorable conditions under which it allows trade in a certain product type to all other WTO members. "Grant someone a special favour and you have to do the same for all other WTO members." National treatment means that imported goods should be treated no less favorably than domestically produced goods (at least after the foreign goods have entered the market) and was introduced to tackle non-tariff barriers to trade (e.g. technical standards, security standards et al. discriminating against imported goods).

2. **Reciprocity**: It reflects both a desire to limit the scope of free-riding that may arise because of the MFN rule, and a desire to obtain better access to foreign markets. A related point is that for a nation to negotiate, it is necessary that the gain from doing so be greater than the gain available from unilateral liberalization; reciprocal concessions intend to ensure that such gains will materialise.

3. **Binding and enforceable commitments**: The tariff commitments made by WTO members in a multilateral trade negotiation and on accession are enumerated in a schedule (list) of concessions. These schedules establish "ceiling bindings": a country can change its bindings, but only after negotiating with its trading partners, which could mean compensating them for loss of trade. If satisfaction is not obtained, the complaining country may invoke the WTO dispute settlement procedures.

4. **Predictable and Transparency**: The WTO members are required to publish their trade regulations, to maintain institutions allowing for the review of administrative decisions affecting trade, to respond to requests for information by other members, and to notify changes in trade policies to the WTO. These internal transparency requirements are supplemented and facilitated by periodic country-specific reports (trade policy reviews) through the Trade Policy Review Mechanism (TPRM). The WTO system tries also to improve predictability and stability, discouraging the use of quotas and other measures used to set limits on quantities of imports. Foreign companies, investors and governments should be confident that trade barriers should not be raised arbitrarily. With stability and predictability, investment is encouraged, jobs are created and consumers can fully enjoy the benefits of competition — choice and lower prices.

5. **Safety valves**: In specific circumstances, governments are able to restrict trade. There are three types of provisions in this direction: articles allowing for the use of trade measures to attain noneconomic objectives; articles aimed at ensuring "fair competition"; and provisions permitting intervention in trade for economic reasons. Exceptions to the MFN principle also allow for preferential treatment of developed countries, regional free trade areas and customs unions.

6. **More competitive**: Discouraging 'unfair' practices, such as export subsidies and dumping products at below cost to gain market share; the issues are complex, and the rules try to establish what is fair or unfair, and how governments can respond, in particular by charging additional import duties calculated to compensate for damage caused by unfair trade.

7. **More beneficial for less developed countries**: Giving them more time to adjust, greater flexibility and special privileges; over three-quarters of WTO members are developing countries and countries in transition to market economies. The WTO agreements give them transition periods to adjust to the more unfamiliar and, perhaps, difficult WTO provisions.

8. **Protect the environment**: The WTO's agreements permit members to take measures to protect not only the environment but also public health, animal health and plant health. However, these measures must be applied in the same way to both national and foreign businesses. In other words, members must not use environmental protection measures as a means of disguising protectionist policies.

Indian Position Vs WTO and Strategies:

India is one of the founding contracting parties to the GATT that was concluded in October 1947. India served as the leader to represents the concerns of the developing countries in the GATT and India has often led the groups of less developed countries in the subsequent Multilateral Trade Negotiations (MTNs) under the auspices of the GATT.

The major issues that India relates itself are - tariff and non-tariff barriers, Quantitative Restrictions (QRs), Trade and Development, reciprocity in trade agreements, and so on.

India's stance at the WTO has undergone a sea change since the beginning of the Uruguay Round of the multilateral trade negotiations. The shifting coordinates of India's position at the WTO focusing on three specific areas of negotiations, namely *agriculture, services and TRIPS*. India's heightened profile at the WTO at the present juncture, along with its economic success and material capability, presents an unprecedented opportunity to use the platform of WTO negotiations as a major foreign policy instrument to play a constructive leadership role.

GATT was as an effort on the part of the developed world faced with mixed fortunes at the end of the war, to discipline themselves in trade in goods and to limit the spread of proactive protectionist policies by individual national governments. India in-principle was supposed to have accepted the mandate, but it remained firm on its trade and development policies aimed at self-reliance and import substitution. The flipside of this protectionist trade policy regime soon revealed itself in the form of inefficiencies of various kinds. For one thing, there was no incentive to keep pace with the fast changing global technology frontier in many of the manufacturing sectors, which resulted in Indian industry becoming technologically backward and inefficient with respect to global standards of costs and quality. From the mid 1980s, a technological view of development started gaining momentum in India's development policy. It was increasingly realized that being able to produce everything could not be the end-all goal. It is very important to be able to do things 'efficiently' as well. That may require opening up the doors to latest technological development on the global frontier, quite a departure from its earlier protectionist policy regime. This, in a sense, marked the beginning of India's policy of liberalization. It was the year 1991 that marked a radical departure from the past when, faced with an exceptionally severe balance of payments crisis, India launched a massive economic reforms package consisting of short-term stabilization measures along with a longer-term program of comprehensive structural reforms. These reforms were much wider and deeper than earlier piecemeal attempts, and which ushered in a complete paradigmatic shift in policymaking that now emphasized not only liberalization of government controls, a larger role for the private sector as the engine of growth, freer operation of market and competitive forces in order to boost efficiency, but greater integration with the world economy through free and unrestricted trade flows.

Interestingly, the Uruguay Round of the GATT negotiations began in 1986, precisely when India's development policy making process was at a watershed. By the time India launched its massive economic reforms package in 1991, marking a paradigm shift in its policy. India's attitude towards the WTO may be best understood against this perspective of the changing mental frame of the Indian policy makers from the mid 1980s onwards, both reinforcing each other. Free trade and greater engagement with the world economy was therefore no more a taboo among Indian policy makers. However, this is not to suggest that the 1991-reforms made India euphoric about the prospects of WTO and its consequences for India. It is natural that the Indian intelligentsia remained rather skeptical about potential vulnerabilities of the nation from the sudden exposure to the world economy. It was only in the area of manufacturing that India's unilateral trade liberalization was carried out during the early1990s. Therefore during the Uruguay Round, India was clearly reluctant to move beyond trade in manufactured goods at the WTO.

India participated in three major Ministerial Meetings, namely Singapore (1996), Geneva (1998) and Seattle (1999). These phases saw multiple instances of loss of mutual confidence among negotiating Partners. All this prompted India to take a hard line on not endorsing a new round at Doha in 2001, arguing that commitments of the Uruguay Round has not been fulfilled and hence it is pointless to initiate a new *round* of negotiating agenda. However, finally India reluctantly signed the Doha Agreement in 2001. At the end, India was quite happy with the Doha outcome, because of its success on three issues: several concessions on implementation issues, weakening of the TRIPS to accommodate access to medicine and public health concerns of developing countries, and most significantly keeping the Singapore Issues at bay. In fact, it was post-Doha that India emerged as a leading and key negotiating partner at the WTO and assumed the role of a pro-active player in the whole process. There was a clear shift from its earlier position of cautious, or at best passive, participation.

To understand the shifting coordinates of India's stance at the WTO, more specifically, one has to examine its position with respect to Agriculture, IPR and Services. These also happen to be some of the most important areas of India's engagement with the WTO.

1. Agriculture

Before the Uruguay, agriculture essentially remained outside the purview of the GATT. GATT in a way allowed export subsidies on agricultural primary products and most certainly allowed import restrictions under certain conditions. Farm lobby politics in developed countries ensured high levels of domestic support for their agricultural sector, completely distorting agricultural trade. The Agreement on Agriculture, which came into force on January 1, 1995, intended to set the ground for a fair and market oriented agricultural trading system with reform programmes comprising of specific commitments to reduce farm support, export subsidies and to promote market access within a stipulated time frame. For India, agriculture is a major area of concern, as it supports the livelihood of 65–70 percent of India's population of 1.02 billion. India continued to pursue its commitment to provide various input subsides to agriculture, concomitant with its policy objectives of food security, rural development, rural employment and crop diversification. Therefore, India's stance on agriculture at the WTO has always been somewhat defensive. It has maintained its demand for flexibilities to carry out with its measures of support for agriculture and rural development and therefore be exempt from any reduction commitments on these counts. Given that agriculture was recognized to be at the heart of the Doha Development Agenda, the Doha Ministerial Declaration flagged off the Doha Round with promises of substantial improvements in agricultural market access and reductions in trade distorting domestic support in agriculture, while paying *equal* attention to developing country concerns.

2. Intellectual Property Rights (IPR)

India's position on making IPR a standard for the Global Trading System has seen a sea change. India's *shifting* stance on IPR at the GATT/WTO spanning over entire period of the Uruguay and the Doha rounds (1986 till date) has drawn a lot of attention in contemporary analysis. India initially had a strong opposition to include Intellectual Property Rights within the ambit of trade negotiations. But over time this defensive approach became more moderate and finally turned somewhat aggressive with respect to specific dimensions.

At the Uruguay Round, developed nations (the US, in particular), under pressure from their pharmaceutical corporate lobby, proposed to introduce a uniformly strong IPR regime on all nations as part of a multilateral trading agreement through the TRIPS agreement. This was in spite of the fact that a strong IPR goes against the core philosophy of the WTO's principle of promoting competition and free trade. Moreover, there is now a large body of theoretical and empirical literature, firmly establishing that IPR regime must be endogenously determined within the economy, depending on the technological learning and capability levels of the country in question. Exogenous imposition of a strong IPR regime may severely hinder the process of technological catch up. Ironically, there is historical evidence to suggest that the developed world has had the flexibility to adopt an appropriate IPR regime during their process of development and technological learning. Countries like Switzerland, Germany, Japan and Italy did not adopt a strong product for a long time. India, beginning in the 1970s and well into the 1980s, was going through a phase of "know-why" oriented technological learning. It was building up process development capabilities through reverse engineering – both infringing process for off-patent items and non-infringing processes for patented ones. This was possible because of its 1970 patent act which allowed only process (and not product patents) on chemical substances.[21] Switching over to strong product patent regime at that point would have put a pre-mature halt to this technological capability building process. The Indian pharmaceutical industry lobby, which was experiencing a phenomenal growth and development based on its process development capabilities (often referred to as the *process revolution*), was extremely apprehensive about the TRIPS agreement. India's strong opposition to TRIPS in the initial years of the Uruguay Round appears to be natural and justified.

A clear shift in India's attitude was visible post-1989. Many believe that this sudden change of stance was a result of trade threats from the US (super 301). Perhaps, it was a merely strategic move for India to adopt this changing stance towards TRIPS in 1989, as a tool for extracting concessions in other aspects of WTO negotiations. But during the 1990s, the domestic business interests also got sharply divided. The associations dominated by MNCs came out openly in support of the TRIPS. Some major domestic players, especially in pharmaceuticals, felt that the technological levels they had reached by then warranted a stronger patent regime for their long run business interests. But a large segment of the domestic industry, still at a nascent stage of technological catch up, continued to pose opposition. Having signed the TRIPS agreement in 1994, India was mandated to change its patent regime by 2005. The domestic pressure was now enormous. Concerns were expressed about the potential increase in drug prices and its adverse effects on access to medicine and public health in India. While the pressure from the industrial lobby was getting weaker and milder compared to what it was in the 1980s, the opposition from the civil society lobby against TRIPS was gaining momentum. This did have an influence on India's position on IPR yet again. At Doha, India along with other developing countries notably Brazil and South Africa (constituting the IBSA group), pushed for an explicit acknowledgement of the primacy of the member countries' rights to protect public health and promote access to affordable medicines. This was achieved in the form of a declaration on TRIPS and public health at Doha that came as major victory for the developing world and an important feather in IBSA's cap at WTO negotiations. The declaration recognizes members' "right to grant compulsory licenses and the freedom to determine the grounds upon which such licenses are granted." Moreover it grants each member the "right to determine what constitutes a national emergency or other circumstances of extreme urgency" in implementing TRIPS.

Two other IPR related issues were raised by India at Doha. First, it wanted to **extend protection under 'geographical indication' (GI)** beyond wine and spirit, to other products. The entire episode of the artificial development of rice variety similar to the Indian *Basmati* rice by the US agro-company Ricetec was under scanner. Second, it **demanded restrictions on misappropriation of biological and genetic resources and traditional knowledge (TK)**.

India's position on TRIPS has remained unchanged post Doha up to Hong Kong. Presently it has focused on three prime concerns – technology transfer, biodiversity and geographical indications. India is of the view that LDCs face serious difficulties in procuring new technologies which could be overcome by suitable safeguards in the domestic IPR laws of LDCs and thereby check the sole rent seeking objectives of the developed country firms in many cases. The other aspect of north-south technology transfer is the growing tendency of intra-firm transfer of technology backed by market seeking motives that relies more on intellectual property protection. This has prompted India to take up the case of technology transfer at the WTO, so that adequate arrangements can be made to ensure such transfers cater to developmental and environmental needs also.

In patenting of organic inventions in terms of micro-organisms and microbiological processes, India proposed harmonization of TRIPS agreement with the UN Convention on Biological Diversity (CBD) and suggested that TRIPS should conform to CBD rather than the other way round. The fault line between the two approaches i.e. CBD and TRIPS, is that CBD considers intellectual property protection as a means to achieving the end of sustainable development, while Agreement on TRIPS considers IPRs as an end in itself. India along with Brazil is at loggerheads with developed countries like the US and Japan in pushing for appropriate amendments in the TRIPS Agreement, to make disclosure of the origin of biological material and traditional knowledge mandatory during filing of patent applications. It should be noted that under present provisions a simple GI protection *per se* does not help preventing 'bio-piracy' since it can only protect the product but not the genetic uniqueness and the traditional knowledge (TK) associated with it.

3. Services

Although trade in services is not essentially a new phenomenon, its explicit recognition as an important component of trade flows is rather recent. Travel, transport and tourism services have always been traded, accounting for significant foreign exchange transactions for many countries. However, a major bulk of services has traditionally been regarded as 'non-tradable.' This perception has undergone a sea change especially with the initiation of the General Agreement on Trade in Services (GATS) under the WTO, with a wide range of services now being actively 'traded' worldwide through new organizational and modal channels. Indeed it during the UR that this new area (services) was brought under the purview of trade negotiations and the outcome was the GATS Agreement that came into force along with the WTO in 1995. GATS classify the provision of services into four modes, namely:

- cross border supply (Mode 1),

- consumption abroad (Mode 2),

- commercial presence (Mode 3); and

- movement of natural persons (Mode 4).

It mandated liberalization of service trade, but adopted a "bottom-up" approach, giving the members full flexibility to undertake trade liberalization in services as per their own priorities and pace, under the provision of 'specific commitments.' Similar to the case of IPR, India, in the initial years of the UR, strongly opposed any proposal for the inclusion of services in the WTO agreement. Indeed during the 1980s, the contribution of services to India's GDP remained quite modest (35–40 percent). It was difficult for Indian policy makers to foresee India's service led growth that the country is experiencing currently.

The upturn of India's services sector began only in the mid-1990s and it has expanded very rapidly in the last decade and a half. Between 1994 and 2004, the services sector grew at the rate of 7.9%, much higher than the growth rates of other sectors as well as that of total GDP (3% for agriculture and allied, 5.3% for manufacturing and 5.9% for total GDP). The share of the services sector in India's GDP increased from 29% in the 1980s to 41% in the 1990s and to 50% in this decade. The expansion of the services sector has been accompanied with a rising trade in services for India. India's share in world services exports almost doubled between 1998–99 and 2004–05 (from 0.99 % to 1.8%). Nearly 50% of India's exports of services are software services. Mode 3 (commercial presence) has been the most important mode, accounting for 57% of India's services trade. The inflow of FDI in services is mostly concentrated in the telecommunications and the financial services sectors. There is also a rising trend in outward FDI (OFDI) in services from India. In fact, services account for 30% of total Indian OFDI. Indian OFDI in services is primarily concentrated in IT and ITES. India's Mode 1 (cross border supply) trade in services, accounting for 28% of India's total services trade, is also dominated by IT and ITES. India's competitive advantage in off-shoring is attributed to its growing pool of highly skilled, low cost workers. The growth in service industry particularly in the high-end software and business services has been immensely facilitated by on-site delivery in many cases in addition to offshore provisioning. Mode 2 (consumption abroad) is gaining importance, especially in areas of health education and tourism. It accounts of 14% of India's total trade in services. Finally, Mode 4 (movement of natural persons) remains an insignificant fraction (1%) of India's total services trade, primarily due to restrictions and regulations on movement of natural persons imposed by member nations. This is one area where trade liberalisation has been resisted the most. Against this backdrop, it is easy to understand how

India, from the mid-1990s, slowly started shifting away from its rigid opposition to service trade and finally by the mid-2000s adopted an aggressive pro-service trade liberalisation posture.

Post 1995, negotiations continued on four major areas of services – financial services, telecom, maritime transport and Mode 4. Agreements on the first two were reached in 1997. India complied without much hesitation and the consequences are evident in terms of a paradigm shift especially in telecom in India, also to some extent in banking. Negotiations on maritime transport were suspended and not much progress was made in the negotiations on Mode 4. India remained, by and large, conservative during the post Uruguay Round negotiations in services, particularly in making commitments in sectors like energy, distribution, environment, education and professional services. In Mode 4, India did not undertake any commitments, like most other members.

Although in the Conditional Initial Offer of January 2004, India was regarded as conservative, in its Revised Offer the very next year, August 2005, India's stance became one of the most ambitious in liberalizing service trade. Not surprisingly, India, by December 2005 had realized its potential gain from service trade liberalization and took an aggressive stance in this regard, even at the cost of annoying and dissociating with some of its long standing developing country allies.

Three sets of indicators point to India's rising power in the WTO:

- participation in the negotiation processes,
- effective use of the Dispute Settlement Mechanism (DSM),
- proven ability to block the negotiation until certain demands are met in meeting after after meeting, negotiators from developed world have reiterated that no deal would be possible without the Indians on board. India acts as a key player in WTO negotiations.

First, it has become a regular invitee and active member of all the small-group decision-making meetings in the WTO where consensus for the plenary meeting is shaped. This is true for meetings at all levels in the WTO – ministerial meetings, heads of delegations meetings, and expert-level meetings. Such meetings usually bring together all those parties which must be on board for an agreement to be reached. India's growing power in the WTO may well be seen as a result of its economic growth also.

Admittedly, India's participation and leadership of coalitions involving developing countries is not new; the fact that it was one of the few developing countries present in the Green Room meetings of the GATT was a product of this leadership. But neither this leadership, nor the entry that it facilitated into Green Room meetings, translated automatically into greater influence in the WTO. It is only much more recently that India has learnt to form effective coalitions that have overcome problems affecting the old coalition types.

4.4: World Intellectual Property Organization WIPO

WIPO was established by the WIPO Convention in 1967 with a mandate from its Member States to promote the protection of IP throughout the world through cooperation among states and in collaboration with other international organizations. It is dedicated to developing a balanced and accessible international intellectual property (IP) system, which rewards creativity, stimulates innovation and contributes to economic development while safeguarding the public interest.

The **World Intellectual Property Organization (WIPO)** is one of the 17 specialized agencies of the United Nations. WIPO was created in 1967 "to encourage creative activity, to promote the protection of intellectual property throughout the world." WIPO currently has 184 member states, administers 24 international treaties and is headquartered in Geneva, Switzerland.

WIPO was formally created by the Convention Establishing the World Intellectual Property Organization, which entered into force on April 26, 1970. Under Article 3 of this Convention, WIPO seeks to "promote the protection of intellectual property throughout the world." WIPO became a specialized agency of the UN in 1974.

The Agreement between the United Nations and the World Intellectual Property Organization notes in Article 1 that WIPO is responsible

> "for promoting creative intellectual activity and for facilitating the transfer of technology related to industrial property to the developing countries in order to accelerate economic, social and cultural development, subject to the competence and responsibilities of the United Nations and its organs, particularly the United Nations Conference on Trade and Development, the United Nations Development Programme and the United Nations Industrial Development Organization, as well as of the United Nations Educational, Scientific and Cultural Organization and of other agencies within the United Nations system."

The Agreement marked a transition for WIPO from the mandate it inherited in 1967 from BIRPI (*Bureaux Internationaux Réunis pour la Protection de la Propriété Intellectuelle,* French acronym for *United International Bureaux for the Protection of Intellectual Property*, which had been established in 1893 to administer the Berne Convention for the Protection of Literary and Artistic Works and the Paris Convention for the Protection of Industrial Property). to promote the protection of intellectual property, to one that involved the more complex task of promoting technology transfer and economic development.

Unlike other branches of the United Nations, WIPO has significant financial resources independent of the contributions from its Member States. In 2006, over 90% of its income of just over CHF 250 million was expected to be generated from the collection of fees by the *International Bureau* (IB) under the intellectual property application and registration systems which it administers (the Patent Cooperation Treaty, the Madrid system for trade marks and the Hague system for industrial designs).

Much of the important work at WIPO is done through committees, including the Standing Committee on Patents (SCP), the Standing Committee on Copyright and Related Rights (SCCR), the Advisory Committee on Enforcement (ACE), and the Intergovernmental Committee (IGC) on Access to Genetic Resources, Traditional Knowledge and Folklore, and the Working Group on Reform of the Patent Cooperation Treaty.

In October 2004, WIPO agreed to adopt a proposal offered by Argentina and Brazil, the "Proposal for the Establishment of a Development Agenda for WIPO" - from the Geneva Declaration on the Future of the World Intellectual Property Organization. This proposal was well supported by developing countries. A number of civil society bodies have been working on a draft Access to Knowledge (A2K) Treaty which they would like to see introduced.

Strategic Goals:

WIPO's revised and expanded strategic goals are part of a comprehensive process of strategic realignment taking place within the Organization. These new goals will enable WIPO to fulfill its mandate more effectively in response to a rapidly evolving external environment, and to the urgent challenges for intellectual property in the 21st Century.

The nine strategic goals were adopted by Member States in the Revised Program and Budget for the 2008/09 Biennium. They are:

- Balanced Evolution of the International Normative Framework for IP

- Provision of Premier Global IP Services

- Facilitating the Use of IP for Development

- Coordination and Development of Global IP Infrastructure

- World Reference Source for IP Information and Analysis

- International Cooperation on Building Respect for IP

- Addressing IP in Relation to Global Policy Issues

- A Responsive Communications Interface between WIPO, its Member States and All Stakeholders

- An Efficient Administrative and Financial Support Structure to Enable WIPO to Deliver its Programs

The Strategic Goals will provide the framework for WIPO's six year Medium Term Strategic Plan (2010 - 2015).

The Washington Post reported in 2003 that Lois Boland (USPTO Director of International Relations) said "that open-source software runs counter to the mission of WIPO, which is to promote intellectual-property rights." Also saying, "To hold a meeting which has as its purpose to disclaim or waive such rights seems to us to be contrary to the goals of WIPO."

Core Activities of WIPO:

The core activities of WIPO are:

1. Development of International IP laws and standards:

WIPO is responsible for promoting the progressive development and harmonization of IP legislation, standards and procedures among its member states. This includes development of international laws and treaties regarding patents, trademarks, industrial designs, geographical indications and copyright and related rights.

WIPO is also working with member states to explore IP issues in the area of traditional knowledge, traditional cultural expressions and genetic resources.

WIPO handles the administration of 24 internatioanl treaties (16 on industrial property, 7 on copyright and the other one the convention creating WIPO).

2. Delivering global IP protection services:

WIPO administers fee-based services, based on international agreements, which enable users in member countries to file international applications for patents (PCT), and international registrations for trademarks (Madrid System), designs (Hague System), and appllations of origin (Libson System).

WIPO administers four IP classification systems, which organize the mass of information concerning inventions, trademarks, and industrial designs into indexed, manageable structures for easy retrieval.

WIPO's Arbitration and Mediation Centre offers dispute resolution srvices to business and individuals, including in the growth area of Internet Domain Name disputes.

3. Encouraging the use of IP for economic development:

WIPO runs a range of programmes aimed at increasing the effective use of IP by developing nations as a tool for economic development. Programmes include technical assistance in support of member countries' initiatives to improve their IP legislative, institutional and human resources framework; strategies for innovation, promotion and IP exploitation; economic studies and material to inform public policy choices.

Contraversy and Criticism:

As with all United Nations multi-government forums, WIPO is not an elected body. WIPO usually attempts to reach decisions by consensus, but in any vote, each Member State is entitled to one vote, regardless of population or contribution to the funding. This factor has led to significant consequences over certain issues, due to the North-South divide in the politics of intellectual property. During the 1960s and 1970s, developing nations were able to block expansions to intellectual property treaties, such as universal pharmaceutical patents which might have occurred through WIPO.

In the 1980s, this led to the United States and other developed countries "forum shifting" intellectual property standard-setting out of WIPO and into the General Agreement on Tariffs and Trade, which later evolved into the World Trade Organization, where the North had greater control of the agenda. This strategy eventually rcsultcd in the enactment of Agreement on Trade-Related Aspects of Intellectual Property Rights (TRIPS).

4.5: Madrid System

The Madrid System, administered by the International Bureau of World Intellectual Property Organization (WIPO), Geneva, permits the filing, registration and maintenance of trademark rights in more than one jurisdiction on a global basis. This system comprises two treaties:

- the Madrid Agreement concerning the International Registration of Marks, which was concluded in 1891 and came into force in 1892 and revised at Brussels (1900), Washington (1911), The Hague (1925), London (1934), Nice (1957), and Stockholm (1967), and amended in 1979; and

- the Protocol relating to the Madrid Agreement, which was concluded in 1989 and came into operation on April 1, 1996 with the aim of rendering the Madrid system more flexible and more compatible with the domestic legislation of certain countries which had not been able to accede to the Agreement.

The Madrid Agreement and the Madrid Protocol were adopted at diplomatic conferences held in Madrid. The Madrid Agreement and Protocol are open to any State which is party to the Paris Convention for the Protection of Industrial Property. The two treaties are parallel and independent and States may adhere to either of them or to both. Any country, which is a member of the Paris Convention of WIPO, can accede to either the Madrid Agreement or the Madrid Protocol or both. Currently, 57 countries are members of the agreement, 77 countries are members of the protocol and 48 countries are members of both the agreement and the protocol. In addition, an intergovernmental organization which maintains its own Office for the registration of marks may become party to the Protocol. Instruments of ratification or accession must be deposited with the Director General of WIPO. States and organizations which are party to the Madrid system are collectively referred to as Contracting Parties.

In legal parlance, the Madrid System provides a mechanism whereby a trademark owner, who has an existing trademark application or registration in a member jurisdiction, may obtain an `international registration' for the trademark from the WIPO. The trademark owner may then extend the protection afforded to the international registration to one or more member jurisdictions through a process known as 'designation.' In other words, the Madrid System "is an international agreement on registration of service and trade marks under which a single application to World Intellectual Property Organization (WIPO) suffices to register a mark in all member countries."

A useful feature of the Madrid System is that this protection may generally be extended to additional jurisdictions at any time, so as to cover geographies that subsequently join the Madrid System, or to such other territories the trademark owner may choose. Additionally, an international mark so registered under the Madrid system is equivalent to an application or a registration of the same mark affected directly in each of the countries designated by the applicant. If the trademark office of a designated country does not refuse protection within a specified period, the protection of the mark is the same as if it had been registered by that office.

Advantages and Disadvantages of Madrid System:

In a nutshell, the primary advantage of the Madrid System is that it allows a trademark owner to obtain protection in any or all member-states by filing one application in one jurisdiction with one set of fees, and make any change — of name, address, etc., — and renew registration across all applicable jurisdictions through a single administrative process. But the one disadvantage of the Madrid System is that any refusal, withdrawal or cancellation of the basic application or basic registration of a trademark within five years of the registration date of the international registration will lead to the refusal, withdrawal or cancellation of the international registration to the same extent.

For instance, if a basic application covers "clothing, headgear and footwear" and "headgear" is deleted for whatever reason, the international registration will only cover "clothing and footwear." The protection afforded by the international registration in each designated member jurisdiction will, therefore, only extend to "clothing and footwear."

*By the same analogy, in this example, if the basic application had been rejected as a whole, the international registration would also be totally refused. The effects of a successful "**central attack**" can be mitigated by transforming the international registration into a series of applications in each jurisdictions designated by the international registration by `**conversion**' process. Although conversion is an expensive option of last resort, the resulting applications will receive the registration date of the international registration as their filing date.*

The costs savings, which usually result from using the Madrid system, are negated by the requirement to use local agents in the applicable jurisdiction if any problem arises.

In today's competitive global market, protection of trademarks and service marks by multinational companies assumes great significance as ownership of a trademark with good image and reputation provides a company with a competitive edge. It enables companies differentiate themselves and their products from those of the competition and thereby plays a pivotal role in brand-building.

There are several advantages in acceding to the protocol instead of the agreement. Accession to the Madrid Protocol will entail amendments to the "Trade Marks Act, 1999."

India and Madrid Protocol on trademark protection:

Further, the importance of the Madrid system may be viewed in terms of the existing trademark laws in India that are territorial in nature and have no international application. Unlike the present Indian patent laws, which provide for international filing of patents under Patent Co-operation Treaty (PCT), registration of one international trademark is not possible under the current trademark laws in India.

Apparently, an important implication of implementing the Madrid system in India will be the requirement of additional staffing in the Trademark Offices and strengthening of IT infrastructure and IT trained personnel, which, presumably, will increase the costs of filing domestic applications. Consequently, the government and local trademark attorneys may lose out, as it would reduce local filings considerably.

Considering the above, though the Madrid Protocol is not the panacea to the problems of national practice, it is the best system now available as, to some extent, it simplifies trademark filings and may reduce costs.

The union cabinet has ratified the country's accession to the Madrid Protocol, which will provide extensive protection to Indian trademarks overseas and facilitate foreign firms to file their trademarks in India. The accession would facilitate speedy registration of Indian marks in different markets worldwide and promote business confidence in the Indian intellectual property rights (IPR) system globally, finance minister of UPA government P Chidambaram told reporters after a meeting of the Cabinet Committee on Economic Affairs (CCEA). He also added that the government would bring a bill in the Parliament for enabling the country's accession to the Madrid Protocol, 1989, which is administered by the World Intellectual Property Organization (WIPO).

The Union Cabinet gave its approval to the following:

- India's accession to the Madrid Protocol concerning the International Registration of Marks,

- Amendment of the Trademarks Act, 1999 with a view to India's accession to the Madrid Protocol concerning the International registration of marks,

- Initiating action for accession to Madrid Protocol and to introduce a Bill in the Parliament.

This will facilitate transfer of technology through trademarks licensing and franchising. This will also facilitate speedy registration of Indian mark in different markets worldwide and promote business confidence in Indian IPR system globally.

The Madrid Protocol vs. the Madrid Agreement:

The earlier discussion makes it clear that the Madrid System for the International Registration of Marks, which is made up of the *Madrid Protocol* and the *Madrid Agreement*. These both establish an administrative process which allows the registration of trademarks in multiple countries by using a single trademark application.

Although almost 100 years younger than the Madrid Agreement, the Madrid Protocol has rapidly overtaken its predecessor in importance.

As per the known details, there are 81 signatories to the Madrid Protocol, which easily outstrips the 56 signatories to the Madrid Agreement. Of the 56 signatories to the Madrid Agreement, only 3 have failed to ratify the Madrid Protocol: Algeria, Kazakhstan and Tajikistan. In contrast, there are quite a few countries which are members of the Madrid Protocol without being members of the Madrid Agreement. These include:

- Australia
- Ireland
- Japan

- The European Union (as a collective body)
- The United Kingdom
- The United States

Further, where a party is bound by both the Madrid Agreement and the Madrid Protocol, only the provisions of the Protocol apply from 1 September 2008 and onwards.

Differences between the Madrid Protocol and the Madrid Agreement:

Use of the Madrid Protocol is slightly less advantageous for applicants than the Madrid Agreement in the following areas:

- **Longer Refusal Periods**: The national trademark offices can refuse to register a Protocol application 18 months from the application date (and longer in the case of refusals based on oppositions) whereas they only have 12 months under the Agreement

- **Higher Fees**: The fees for Protocol Applications are slightly higher than for Agreement Applications, although they are still much less than filing direct national applications

Importantly, the Madrid Protocol has introduced a number of advantages for trademark owners. These include:

- **Language**: Madrid Agreement Applications must be in French, whereas Protocol Applications may be in French, English or Spanish (which is obviously an advantage in non-French speaking jurisdictions

- **Timing**: Protocol Applications can be based upon either an existing trademark registration or a pending application, whereas Agreement Applications can only be based on existing registrations. Therefore, international protection can be sought at a much earlier stage;

- **Coverage**: As explained above, protection is available under the Protocol in some 25 additional countries, including very important markets such as the United States, the United Kingdom and Japan; and

- **The Presence of a "Plan B"**: If the basic trademark application is refused, withdrawn or cancelled, a Madrid Protocol registration can be converted into national applications without losing the original filing date (although this is quite expensive).

4.6: Hague Agreement

(Hague Agreement Concerning the International Deposit of Industrial Designs):

The **Hague Agreement Concerning the International Deposit of Industrial Designs**, also known as the *Hague system* provides a mechanism for registering an industrial design in several countries by means of a single application, filed in one language, with one set of fees. The system is administered by WIPO.

The Geneva Act traces its roots to, and revises, the **Hague Agreement Concerning the International Deposit of Industrial Designs** done at the Hague, Netherlands on November 6, 1925, which entered into force in 1928, and was subsequently revised numerous times. The most significant of these previous revisions were the London Act of 1934 and the Hague Act of 1960 and the Geneva Act of July 2, 1999.

[The original Hague Agreement and its previous acts, however, did not meet the needs of countries, such as the United States, that require a substantive examination of designs for novelty and non-obviousness. Accordingly, the United States never became a party to the original Hague Agreement or its earlier versions.

Thus, the Geneva Act was negotiated with the needs of examining offices, such as the USPTO, in mind. This Act allows the United States to have the benefits of a multinational design protection system while preserving the substantive examination system of the United States.]

Contracting Parties and Qualification to use the Hague system:

Applicants can qualify to use the Hague system on the basis of any of the following criteria:

- the applicant is a national of a Contracting Party (i.e. member country)

- the applicant is domiciled in a Contracting Party

- the applicant has a real and effective industrial or commercial establishment in a Contracting Party

- the applicant has its habitual residence in a Contracting Party (only available if the Contracting Party in question has adhered to the 1999 (Geneva) Act)

An applicant who does not qualify under one of these headings cannot use the Hague system. The Contracting Parties include not only individual countries, but also intergovernmental organisations such as the ***African Intellectual Property Organization (OAPI)*** and the ***European Union***. This means an applicant domiciled in an EU member country that is not a Contracting Party, such as Austria or the United Kingdom, can nevertheless use the Hague system on the basis of his or her domicile in the European Union.

Mode of Filing Application and Registration procedure:

An application may be filed in English, French, or Spanish, at the choice of the applicant. The application must contain one or more views of the designs concerned and can include up to 100 different designs provided that the designs are all in the same class of the International Classification of Industrial Designs (Locarno Classification).

The application fee is composed of three types of fees:

- basic fee,

- publication fee,

- designation fee for each designated Contracting Party.

The application is examined for formal requirements by the International Bureau of WIPO, which provides the applicant with the opportunity to correct certain irregularities in the application. Once the formal requirements have been met, it is recorded in the International Register and details are published electronically in the International Designs Bulletin on the WIPO website.

If any designated Contracting Party considers that a design which has been registered for protection in that Contracting Party does not meet its domestic criteria for registrability (e.g. it finds that the design is not novel), it must notify the International Bureau that it refuses the registration for that Contracting Party. In every Contracting Party that does not issue such a refusal, the international registration takes effect and provides the same protection as if the design(s) had been registered under the domestic law of that Contracting Party.

The duration of an international registration is five years, extendable in further five-year periods up to the maximum duration permitted by each Contracting Party. Renewals are handled centrally by the International Bureau. The applicant pays a renewal fee and notifies the International Bureau of the countries for which the registration is to be renewed.

4.7: The Berne Convention for the Protection of Literary and Artistic Works, 1886

The Berne Convention for the Protection of Literary and Artistic Works (hereinafter referred to as the Convention) is the oldest international agreement in the field of copyright. Copyright is the protection given by the law to original literary and artistic works. The Convention is the most important treaty that governs the area of copyright.

The Convention was signed in 1886 and has been revised several times. These revisions typically occur at twenty-year intervals, however, the last revision was done in Paris in 1971. The Paris 1971 Revision was notable because it added to the Convention the Appendix containing the Special Provisions Regarding Developing Countries.

The adoption of the Convention was prompted by the need to bring uniformity to the disparate bilateral treaties that existed in the nineteenth century. The importance of the Convention was increased when the United States of America abandoned the rival Universal Copyright Convention (administered by the United Nations Educational Scientific and Cultural Organization) and joined the Convention.

Another boost for the Convention came with the signing of the Agreement on Trade Related Aspects of Intellectual Property Rights (TRIPS). Contracting States of the TRIPS Agreement are mandated to implement certain substantive provisions of the Convention.

The Berne Convention

Article 1 of the Convention established a Union of Member States of the Convention, with the aim of protecting the rights of creators of literary and artistic works. The Convention also established an administrative secretariat known as the "***International Bureau.***" This secretariat later amalgamated with the secretariat established by the Paris Convention and the resulting combined secretariat later became the World Intellectual Property Organization (WIPO).

Works Protected by the Convention:

The expression "literary and artistic works" is defined as including every production in the literary, scientific and artistic domain, irrespective of the mode or form of the production's expression. This expression is general in the sense that it encompasses every original work of authorship, regardless of the work's literary or artistic merit. According to Article 2 (1) of the Convention, literary and artistic works include-

> "books, pamphlets and other writings; lectures, addresses, sermons and other works of the same nature; dramatic or dramatico-musical works; choreographic works or entertainments in dumb show; musical compositions with or without words; cinematographic works to which are assimilated works expressed by a process analogous to cinematography; works of drawing, painting, architecture, sculpture, engraving and lithography; photographic works to which are assimilated works expressed by a process analogous to photography; works of applied art; illustrations, maps, plans, sketches and three Essential Elements of Intellectual Property, Overview of the Basic Notions of Copyright and Related Rights and Treaties Administered by WIPO, CD-ROM published by the WIPO Academy, World Intellectual Property Organization, dimensional works relative to geography, topography, architecture or science."

The list outlined in Article 2 (1) of the Convention is not a closed list. A good illustration of this point can be found in the emergence of computer programs in the field of copyright protection. Computer programs have been defined as a set of instructions that direct the operations of a computer and command the computer to perform tasks such as storage and retrieval of information. Although computer programs were never included in the Convention's list of protected works, it is crystal clear that such works are covered by the expression "every production in the literary, scientific and artistic domain."

Other examples of works which were not included in the Convention's list but which are now under the umbrella of copyright are multimedia productions. The jury is still out on an acceptable legal definition of a multimedia production, however, there is a general acceptance "that the combination of sound, text and images in a digital format which is made accessible by a computer program, embodies an original expression of authorship sufficient to justify the protection of multimedia productions under the umbrella of copyright."

The list of works protected by copyright also includes translations, adaptations, arrangements of music and other alterations of literary and artistic works, and collections of literary and artistic works (such as encyclopaedias and anthologies) which constitute intellectual creations, and which do not prejudice the copyright in the original works.

Member States are free to decide how, and the conditions under which, their copyright laws will apply to works of applied art and industrial designs and models.

News items and other items of press information are not eligible for protection under the Convention. The issue of whether political speeches and speeches given during legal proceedings are protected under the Convention is left for determination by the legislation of countries of the Union. The conditions under which public lectures, addresses and other similar works are incorporated in press reports and communicated to the public for informatory purposes, is also reserved for determination by the legislation of countries of the Union.

The author of a political speech or a speech given during legal proceedings, or a public lecture, address or other similar work, shall always enjoy the exclusive right to make a collection of his or her works. The protection of the above-mentioned works shall operate for the benefit of the author and his or her successors in title.

The Convention excludes from the definition of publication, the performance of a dramatic, dramatico-musical, cinematographic or musical work; the public recitation of a literary work; the communication by wire or the broadcasting of a literary or artistic work; the exhibition of a work of art and the construction of a work of architecture.

Principles of the Convention:

The author of a work protected under the Convention is entitled in countries of the Union, other than the country of origin of his or her work, to the same rights granted to nationals of such countries and to the rights granted by this Convention. This principle is known as the principle of national treatment, and is one of the three core principles enshrined in the Convention. The other two principles are the lack of formalities for copyright protection and the independence of copyright protection from the existence or term of protection in the country of origin of the protected work.

The rights granted to authors shall not be subject to formalities such as registration. The most notable exception to this principle is the United States of America. Although the United States of America is a country of the Union, it has a copyright system that requires American works to be registered with the Copyright Office of the Library of Congress, and the printing of the reserved-rights notice on copies of the work. The reserved-right notice includes the circled letter 'c', followed by the year of first publication of the work.

The scope of the rights of the author, as well as the remedies open to the author, are determined exclusively by the laws of the country where the author claims protection. The existence of protection in the country of origin of the work shall have no bearing on such determination. The principle of national treatment is also extended to cases in which the author is not a national of the country of origin of his or her work, in such cases; the author is entitled to the same protection as nationals of such countries.

The Country of Origin:

The Convention provides several definitions of the expression "country of origin."

- If the work is first published in a country of the Union, that country is the country of origin.

- If a work is published simultaneously in several countries of the Union, which have different terms of protection, the country of origin is the country with the shortest term of protection.

- Where the work is published simultaneously in a country of the Union and a non-Union country, the country of origin is the country of the Union.

- If the work in question is an unpublished work, or a work first published in a non-Union country without simultaneous publication in a Union country, the country of origin is the Union country of which the author is a national. However, this last rule does not apply in the case of a cinematographic work made by a person whose headquarters or habitual residence is in a Union country, or a work of architecture built in a Union country, or other artistic works incorporated in a structure located in a Union country. In such cases, the country of origin is the Union country in which the person's headquarters or habitual residence, or the work of architecture or structure, is located.

If a Union country exercises its right to restrict the protection it gives to the works of authors from countries that do not adequately protect the rights of the Union country's nationals, other Union countries shall not be required to grant wider protection to such works. The restrictions imposed by the Union country shall not have retrospective effect, and the Union countries imposing such restrictions are obliged to notify the Director General of WIPO (hereinafter referred to as "the Director General") of the countries affected by such restrictions and the particular restrictions imposed. The Director General shall immediately communicate this notification to all Union countries.

Moral Rights:

The author of a work has the right to be identified as the author of the work (***right of paternity***), and the right to object to any derogatory treatment of his or her work that will be harmful to his or her honour or reputation (***right of integrity***). These rights are known as moral (non-patrimonial) rights and are distinct from the author's economic (patrimonial) rights. Moral rights deal with the author's personal relationship with his or her work.

The **right of paternity** is basically the right to claim authorship of the work. This involves the right of the author to have his or her name mentioned, within reasonable limits, when the work is reproduced. An exception to this rule lies in the fact that a disc jockey is not expected to announce the name of the composer, lyric writer, arranger, etc., of every record he or she plays in a discotheque.

The **right of integrity** on the other hand involves the right of the author to object to any distortion of his or her work, which will affect the author's literary and artistic reputation. A good illustration can be found in the objection by the author of a non-pornographic novel to the adaptation of the novel into a pornographic film.

Moral rights are usually unaffected by the transfer of the author's economic rights. This is due to the personal nature of moral rights. It is not unusual for the economic rights in a work to belong to one person (for example, a film producer or a publisher) and the moral rights to belong to someone else (the individual creator of a film script or novel).

The laws of the country where protection is claimed shall determine the means of redress open to owners of moral rights. Infringements of moral rights are usually actionable as contraventions of copyright and the persons entitled to such moral rights are deemed to be the owners of the copyright in question. Infringements of moral rights may also give rise to infringement of personality rights at common law.

Terms of Protection:

The general term of copyright protection granted by the Convention is the life of the author and fifty years from the end of the year of his death. The Convention then gives certain specific terms of protection for certain categories of works.

In the case of cinematographic works, the term of protection is fifty years from the end of year in which the work became available to the public with the author's consent. If the cinematographic work has not been made available to the public within fifty years from the making of the work, the term of protection shall be fifty years from the end of the year of such making.

The term of protection for anonymous and pseudonymous works is fifty years from the end of the year in which the work became lawfully available to the public. If the identity of the author of an anonymous or pseudonymous work is revealed to the public, the general term of protection will apply. Where there is a reasonable presumption that the author of an anonymous or pseudonymous work has been dead for fifty years, the obligation of Union countries to protect such a work shall lapse.

Countries of the Union are given the discretion to prescribe the terms of protection of photographic works and works of applied art protected as artistic works. However, the minimum term of protection of a photographic work, or a work of applied art protected as an artistic work shall extend to the end of a period of twenty-five years calculated from the making of such work.

Countries of the Union are free to grant terms of protection that are longer than those provided by the Convention. The term of protection of a work shall not exceed the term fixed by the country of origin of the work, unless otherwise prescribed by the law of the country where protection is claimed.

In the case of works of joint authorship, the terms of protection counted from the death of the author are calculated from the death of the last surviving author.

Exclusive Rights and Exceptions:

Translation and Reproduction:

The Convention gives authors of literary and artistic works the exclusive right to translate or authorize translations of their works during the term of protection of their original works. Translation refers to the expression of a work in a language that is different from the language of the original version. The Convention also gives authors of literary and artistic works the exclusive right to authorize all types of reproduction of their works. The reproduction right is basically the exclusive right of the copyright owner to make copies of the protected work. This exclusive right of reproduction has been described as the most basic right under copyright.

Special Exceptions:

Countries of the Union are free to legislate exceptions to the reproduction right in certain special cases. However, such exceptions should not conflict with a normal exploitation of the work and should not unreasonably prejudice the author's legitimate interests.

Countries of the Union are free to enact legislation or conclude special agreements allowing the utilization of literary or artistic works in the form of illustration in publications, broadcasts or sound or visual recordings for teaching. However, the extent of such utilization should not exceed that justified by the purpose and should not be incompatible with fair practice. Where the work of an author is quoted or utilized as illustrations for teaching, the source, and the name (if it appears on the work), of the author shall be mentioned.

Countries of the Union may allow articles published in the print media on current economic, political or religious topics, and broadcasted works on such topics, to be reproduced by the press, broadcasted or communicated to the public by wire. However, such reproduction, broadcasting or communication should not be allowed if it has been expressly reserved by the owner, and the source of the work must always be clearly indicated.

Works Situated in Public Places

The countries of the Union are also free to legislate the conditions under which the reporting of current events by means of photography, cinematography, broadcasting or communication to the public by wire may incorporate (to an extent justified by informatory purposes) literary or artistic works seen or heard during the event.

Public Performance and Other Communication to the Public

The Convention gives authors of dramatic, dramatico-musical and musical works the exclusive right of authorizing any type of public performance of their works and any communication to the public of performances of their works. A public performance of a work has been described as "any performance of a work at a place where the public is or can be present, or at a place not open to the public, but where a substantial number of persons outside the normal circle of a family and its closest social acquaintances is present." Authors of dramatic or dramatico-musical works are also given the exclusive right of authorizing translations of their works during the terms of protection of such works.

According to Article 11bis(1) of the Convention, countries of the Union are obliged to give authors of literary and artistic works the exclusive right of authorizing-

i. "the broadcasting of their works and the communication thereof to the public by any other means of wireless diffusion of signs, sounds or images;

ii. any communication to the public by wire or by rebroadcasting of the broadcast of the work, when this communication is made by an organization other than the original one;

iii. the public communication by loudspeaker or any other analogous instrument transmitting, by signs, sounds or images, the broadcast of the work."

Union countries are free to determine the conditions under which the rights referred to in Article 11bis (1) shall be exercised; however, such conditions shall only apply in the countries that have prescribed them. Further, such conditions shall not prejudice the moral rights of the author or the author's right to obtain an equitable remuneration.

Unless otherwise stipulated, an authorization granted by virtue of Article 11bis(1) does not include a permission to record the broadcasted work by means of audio or visual equipment. Countries of the Union may also determine the regulations governing ephemeral (temporary) recordings made by means of the facilities of a broadcasting organization for the broadcasts of the organization. Such regulations may also permit the Article 11bis(2) preservation of ephemeral recordings of exceptional documentary character in official archives.

Adaptations and Other Alterations

The Convention gives authors of literary and artistic works the exclusive right of authorizing adaptations, arrangements and other alterations of their works. An adaptation of a work occurs when the work is modified in order to create another work. A good example can be found in the adaptation of a novel into a movie. Such an adaptation occurred when Alex Haley's best-selling novel, "Roots," was modified into a television series of the same name. Further, authors of literary and artistic works are also given the exclusive right of authorizing-

i. "the cinematographic adaptation and reproduction of these works, and the distribution of the works thus adapted or reproduced;

ii. the public performance and communication to the public by wire of the works thus adapted or reproduced."

A person wishing to adapt a cinematographic work derived from a literary or artistic work, into another artistic work, must seek the authorization of both the author of the literary or artistic work and the author of the cinematographic work derived from the literary or artistic work.

"DROIT DE SUITE":

The author of an original work of art or an original manuscript, or his or her personal representatives, shall always enjoy an inalienable right to an interest in any sale of the work, after the first transfer by the author of the work. This right is given to copyright owners and their heirs by the laws of countries such as France. This right is founded on the rationale that copyright owners are frequently unable to sell their works for a fair price at the time such works were created. However, the value of such works can appreciate to very high levels in the future. A good *example* of such an unfortunate copyright owner is the famous Dutch painter, **Van Gogh**. During his lifetime, he had great trouble selling his works, however, his works now sell for millions of pounds.

This protection is dependent on whether the author's country provides for such a protection, and to the extent permitted by the country where the author claims such protection. Countries are free to determine, by national legislation, the amount of such an interest and the procedure for collecting the amount.

Enforcement of Protected Rights:

For a person to be regarded, in the absence of proof to the contrary, as the author of a literary or artistic work, and also to be entitled to institute infringement proceedings in countries of the Union, that person's name must appear on the work in the usual manner. This provision also applies to authors using pseudonyms that leave no doubt as to the identity of the author.

According to Article 15 (3) of the Convention, if the identity of the author of an anonymous or pseudonymous work is not known, the publisher whose name is indicated on the work shall, in the absence of proof to the contrary, be entitled to enforce the author's rights as the representative of the author.

Where there is a strong presumption that a national of a Union country is the author of an anonymous unpublished work, the Union country shall be free to designate, in its national legislation, the competent authority that shall be entitled to enforce the author's rights in the countries of the Union. Any Union country that makes such a designation shall issue a written declaration to the Director General giving full details concerning the designated competent authority. The Director General shall immediately communicate this notification to all Union countries.

Countries of the Union are empowered to seize infringing copies of any work that enjoys protection in such countries. Infringing copies of such works imported from a country that does not protect the work are also liable to seizure.

Greater Protection and Special Agreements:

The Convention does not prejudice any claim to any greater protection provided for in the copyright legislation of any Union country. According to Article 20 of the Convention, countries of the Union are also free to enter into special agreements, among themselves, which grant authors more protection than those granted by the Convention or which do not contradict the provisions of the Convention. The Convention also saves existing agreements that satisfy these criteria. Major investigations of the position of copyright material on information superhighways were launched…internationally… at WIPO."

These investigations focused on extending the scope of the Convention because of the rapid advances in technology. It is no wonder that the WCT and the other product of these investigations, the WIPO Performances and Phonograms Treaty (WPPT), are jointly referred to as the WIPO Internet Treaties.

Special Provisions Regarding Developing Countries:

The Convention includes certain special provisions regarding developing countries in the Appendix that is attached to the Convention. These provisions resulted from the clamour by developing countries during the 1960s for more changes to the Convention. As stated earlier, the Appendix was added to the Convention by the Paris 1971 Revisions of the Convention.

Countries classified as developing countries by the United Nations which accept the Convention, may notify the Director General of WIPO at the time of depositing their instrument of ratification or accession, or may at any time after such deposit declare, that they are availing themselves of the provisions of Article II or III or of both these Articles. Such a country may instead of relying on the provisions of Article II, make a declaration under Article V (1)(a). A country making a declaration under Article V is barred from subsequently relying on the provisions of Article II, even if it withdraws the declaration under Article V.

If the Director General is notified of such a declaration before the expiration of a period of ten years calculated from the commencement of Articles 1 to 21 and the Appendix, the declaration shall be effective until the expiration of the ten-year period. A country availing itself of the provisions of Article II or III may renew its declaration (wholly or partly) for successive ten-year periods by depositing a notification with the Director General. Such notification should be deposited within a period of not more than fifteen months and not less than three months before the expiration of the existing ten-year period.

If the Director General is notified of the declaration after the expiration of a period of ten years calculated from the commencement of Articles 1 to 21 and the Appendix, the declaration shall be effective until the expiration of the existing ten-year period. Such a declaration may also renewed for periods of ten years each by notifying the Director General within a period of not more than fifteen months and not less than three months before the expiration of the existing ten-year period.

The Convention can best be described as the most versatile international agreement in the arena of copyright law. As was stated earlier, the Convention protects a host of literary and artistic works thereby ensuring that the creators of these protected works recover some compensation for the time, money, effort and thought they invested into the creation of such works. This protection has fostered the growth of copyright industries such as the music industry into multi-billion dollar businesses.

This success of the music industry has not only benefited developed countries but also developing countries as well. The popularity of "world music" is a testament to this fact. World music is a brand of music from the developing world involving the fusion of traditional music and modern pop music.

The importance of effectively protecting intellectual property is eloquently summed up in the inscription on the cupola of the headquarters of WIPO-

*"**Human genius is the source of all works of art…these works are the guarantee of a life worthy of men. It is the duty of the State to ensure with diligence the protection of the arts…..**"*

The Convention is surely one of the best weapons in the armory of copyright protection.

4.8: Paris Convention for the Protection of Industrial Property

The **Paris Convention for the Protection of Industrial Property**, signed in Paris, France, on March 20, 1883, was one of the first intellectual property treaties. It established a Union for the protection of industrial property. The Convention is still in force as of February 2012. Countries that did so formed themselves into a "Union" of patenting authorities, and are sometimes referred to as the "Paris Union." The document itself is known as the "Paris Convention" for short.

After a diplomatic conference in Paris in 1880, the Convention was signed in 1883 by 11 countries: Belgium, Brazil, France, Guatemala, Italy, the Netherlands, Portugal, El Salvador, Serbia, Spain and Switzerland and ratified in 1884.

The Treaty was revised at Brussels, Belgium, on December 14, 1900, at Washington, United States, on June 2, 1911, at The Hague, Netherlands, on November 6, 1925, at London, United Kingdom, on June 2, 1934, at Lisbon, Portugal, on October 31, 1958, and at Stockholm, Sweden, on July 14, 1967, and was amended on September 28, 1979.

As of December 2011, the Convention has 174 contracting member countries, which makes it one of the most widely adopted treaties worldwide. Notably, Taiwan and Kuwait are not parties to the Convention. However, according to Article 27 of its Patent Act, Taiwan recognizes priority claims from contracting members. The Paris Convention will enter into force in Brunei Darussalam on 17 February 2012, bringing the total number of Nation States party to the Convention to 174.

The Convention applies to industrial property in the widest sense, including patents, marks, industrial designs, utility models (a kind of "small patent" provided for by the laws of some countries), trade names (designations under which an industrial or commercial activity is carried on), geographical indications (indications of source and appellations of origin) and the repression of unfair competition.

[Contracting parties:

Contracting members include: Albania; Algeria; Andorra; Angola; Antigua and Barbuda; Argentina; Armenia; Australia; Austria; Azerbaijan; Bahamas; Bahrain; Bangladesh; Barbados; Belarus; Belgium; Belize; Benin; Bhutan; Bolivia; Bosnia and Herzegovina; Botswana; Brazil; Brunei Darussalam, Bulgaria; Burkina Faso; Burundi; Cambodia; Cameroon; Canada; Central African Republic; Chad; Chile; China; Colombia; Comoros; Congo; Costa Rica; Croatia; Cuba; Cyprus; Czech Republic; Côte d'Ivoire; Democratic People's Republic of Korea; Democratic Republic of the Congo; Denmark; Djibouti; Dominica; Dominican Republic; Ecuador; Egypt; El Salvador; Equatorial Guinea; Estonia; Finland; France; Gabon; Gambia; Georgia; Germany; Ghana; Greece; Grenada; Guatemala; Guinea; Guinea-Bissau; Guyana; Haiti; Holy See; Honduras; Hungary; Iceland; India; Indonesia; Iran (Islamic Republic of); Iraq; Ireland; Israel; Italy; Jamaica; Japan; Jordan; Kazakhstan; Kenya; Kyrgyzstan; Laos; Latvia; Lebanon; Lesotho; Liberia; Libya; Liechtenstein; Lithuania; Luxembourg; Macedonia;[3] Madagascar; Malawi; Malaysia; Mali; Malta; Mauritania; Mauritius; Mexico; Moldova; Monaco; Mongolia; Morocco; Mozambique; Namibia; Nepal; Netherlands; New Zealand; Nicaragua; Niger; Nigeria; Norway; Oman; Pakistan; Panama; Papua New Guinea; Paraguay; Peru; Philippines; Poland; Portugal; Qatar; Republic of Korea; Romania; Russian

Federation; Rwanda; Saint Kitts and Nevis; Saint Lucia; Saint Vincent and the Grenadines; San Marino; Sao Tome and Principe; Saudi Arabia; Senegal; Serbia; Seychelles; Sierra Leone; Singapore; Slovakia; Slovenia; South Africa; Spain; Sri Lanka; Sudan; Suriname; Swaziland; Sweden; Switzerland; Syrian Arab Republic; Tajikistan; Thailand; Togo; Tonga; Trinidad and Tobago; Tunisia; Turkey; Turkmenistan; Uganda; Ukraine; United Arab Emirates; United Kingdom; United Republic of Tanzania; United States of America; Uruguay; Uzbekistan; Venezuela; Vietnam; Yemen; Zambia; and Zimbabwe.]

Provisions of the Convention:

The substantive provisions of the Convention fall into three main categories: national treatment, right of priority, common rules.

1. National treatment:

According to Articles 2 and 3 of this treaty, juristic and natural persons who are either national of or domiciled in a state party to the Convention shall, as regards the protection of industrial property, enjoy in all the other countries of the Union, the advantages that their respective laws grant to nationals.

In other words, when an applicant files an application for a patent or a trademark in a foreign country member of the Union, the application receives the same treatment as if it came from a national of this foreign country. Furthermore, if the intellectual property right is granted (e.g. if the applicant becomes owners of a patent or of a registered trademark), the owner benefits from the same protection and the same legal remedy against any infringement as if the owner was a national owner of this right.

Nationals of non-contracting States are also entitled to national treatment under the Convention if they are domiciled or have a real and effective industrial or commercial establishment in a contracting State.

2. Priority right:

The "Convention *priority right,*" also called "Paris Convention priority right" or "Union priority right," was also established by Article 4 of this treaty. It provides that an applicant from one contracting State shall be able to use its first filing date (in one of the contracting State) as the effective filing date in another contracting State, provided that the applicant files another application within 6 months (for industrial designs and trademarks) or 12 months (for patents and utility models) from the first filing.

To be more specific, the industrial property right is granted for a fixed period of time by a country. The date from which right is deemed to start is usually the date of filing of complete specification. To obtain rights in other member countries, the application must be filed on the same day in the member countries if it is desired to have the rights started from the same day. However, there are practical difficulties in synchronizing the activities. For facilitating simultaneous protection in member countries, the Convention provides that with in 12 months of national filing, if patent applications are filed in member countries, the patents, if granted in member countries, will be effective from that date of national filing. This right is known as the 'right of priority.'

In case the applicant after a second look at the patent application finds that the patent contains more than one invention or on his own accord wishes to divide the application, he can claim the initial date of priority for subsequent patent applications.

The applicant may also, on his own initiative, divide a patent application and preserve as the date of each divisional application and the benefit of the right of priority, if any. Each country of the Union shall have the right to determine the conditions under which such division shall be authorized.

Priority may not be refused on the ground that certain elements of the invention for which priority is claimed do not appear among the claims formulated in the application in the country of origin, provided that the application documents as a whole specifically disclose such elements. (India presently has priority arrangements with 72 countries).

3. Common Rules:

The Convention lays down a few common rules which all the contracting States must follow. The more important are the following:

(a) As to Patents:

Patents granted in different contracting States for the same invention are independent of each other: the granting of a patent in one contracting State does not oblige the other contracting States to grant a patent; a patent cannot be refused, annulled or terminated in any contracting State on the ground that it has been refused or annulled or has terminated in any other contracting State. In otherwords, granting a patent in one country of the Union does not force other countries to grant the patent for the same invention. And, the refusal of the patent in one country does not mean that it will be terminated in all the countries.

The inventor has the right to be named as such in the patent.

The grant of a patent may not be refused, and a patent may not be invalidated, on the ground that the sale of the patented product, or of a product obtained by means of the patented process, is subject to restrictions or limitations resulting from the domestic law.

Each contracting State that takes legislative measures providing for the grant of **compulsory licenses to prevent the abuses which might result from the exclusive rights conferred by a patent may do so only with certain limitations**. Thus, a compulsory license (license not granted by the owner of the patent but by a public authority of the State concerned) based on failure to work the patented invention may only be granted pursuant to a request filed after three or four years of failure to work or insufficient working of the patented invention and it must be refused if the patentee gives legitimate reasons to justify his inaction. Furthermore, forfeiture of a patent may not be provided for, except in cases where the grant of a compulsory license would not have been sufficient to prevent the abuse. In the latter case, proceedings for forfeiture of a patent may be instituted, but only after the expiration of two years from the grant of the first compulsory license.

(b) As to Marks:

The Paris Convention does not regulate the conditions for the filing and registration of marks which are therefore determined in each contracting State by the domestic law. Consequently, no application for the registration of a mark filed by a national of a contracting State may be refused, nor may a registration be invalidated, on the ground that filing, registration or renewal has not been effected in the country of origin. Once the registration of a mark is obtained in a contracting State, it is independent of its possible registration in any other country, including the country of origin; consequently, the lapse or annulment of the registration of a mark in one contracting State will not affect the validity of registration in other contracting States.

Where a mark has been duly registered in the country of origin, it must, on request, be accepted for filing and protected in its original form in the other contracting States. Nevertheless, registration may be refused in well-defined cases, such as when the mark would infringe acquired rights of third parties, when it is devoid of distinctive character, when it is contrary to morality or public order, or when it is of such a nature as to be liable to deceive the public.

If, in any contracting State, the use of a registered mark is compulsory, the registration cannot be canceled until after a reasonable period, and only if the owner cannot justify his inaction.

Each contracting State must refuse registration and prohibit the use of marks which constitute a reproduction, imitation or translation, liable to create confusion, of a mark considered by the competent authority of that State to be well known in that State as being already the mark of a person entitled to the benefits of the Convention and used for identical or similar goods.

Each contracting State must likewise refuse registration and prohibit the use of marks which consist of or contain without authorization, armorial bearings, State emblems and official signs and hallmarks of contracting states, provided they have been communicated through the International Bureau of WIPO. The same provisions apply to armorial bearings, flags, other emblems, abbreviations and names of certain intergovernmental organizations.

Collective marks must be granted protection.

(c) As to Industrial Designs:

Industrial designs must be protected in each contracting State, and protection may not be forfeited on the ground that the articles incorporating the design are not manufactured in that State.

(d) As to Trade Names:

Protection must be granted to trade names in each contracting State without the obligation of filing or registration.

(e) As to Indications of Source:

Measures must be taken by each contracting State against direct or indirect use of a false indication of the source of the goods or the identity of the producer, manufacturer or trader.

(f) As to Unfair Competition:

Each contracting State must provide for effective protection against unfair competition. Any act of competition contrary to honest practices in industrial or commercial matters constitutes an act of unfair competition. It has been made mandatory for the member countries of the TRIPs Agreement to comply with the Article 1 to 12 and Article 19 of the Paris Convention.

Advantages of Joining the Paris Convention:

There are number of international conventions and treaties which are open only to the members of the Paris Convention. Some of them are the benefits from:

- Patent Cooperation Treaty (PCT),
- Budapest Treaty (for deposit of microorganisms),
- UPOV (Union for Protection Of new Varieties of plants)
- Madrid Agreement and Madrid Protocol,
- Hague Agreement, etc.

The Paris Union, established by the Convention, has an Assembly and an Executive Committee. Every State member of the Union which has adhered to at least the administrative and final provisions of the Stockholm Act (1967) is a member of the Assembly. The members of the Executive Committee are elected from among the members of the Union, except for Switzerland, which is a member *ex officio*. The establishment of the biennial program and budget of the WIPO Secretariat—as far as the Paris Union is concerned—is the task of its Assembly.

The Convention is open to all States. Instruments of ratification or accession must be deposited with the Director General of WIPO.

4.9: Budapest Treaty

The **Budapest Treaty on the International Recognition of the Deposit of Microorganisms for the Purposes of Patent Procedure**, or **Budapest Treaty**, is an international treaty signed in Budapest, Hungary, on April 28, 1977. It entered into force on August 9, 1980, and was later amended on September 26, 1980. The treaty is administered by the World Intellectual Property Organization (WIPO).

As of June 2011, 75 countries were party to the Budapest Treaty. The Budapest Treaty will enter into force with respect to Morocco, the 74th contracting state, on 20 July 2011. The accession to the Treaty is open to States party to the Paris Convention for the Protection of Industrial Property of 1883. The African Regional Industrial Property Organization (ARIPO), the Eurasian Patent Organization (EAPO) and the European Patent Organisation (EPO) have filed a declaration of acceptance under Article 9(1)(a) of the Treaty.

The treaty allows "deposits of microorganisms at an international depositary authority to be recognized for the purposes of patent procedure." Usually, in order to meet the legal requirement of sufficiency of disclosure, patent applications and patents must disclose in their description the subject-matter of the invention in a manner sufficiently clear and complete to be carried out by the person skilled in the art (see also: reduction to practice). When an invention involves a microorganism, completely describing said invention in the description to enable third parties to carry it out is usually impossible. This is why, in the particular case of inventions involving microorganisms, a deposit of biological material must be made in a recognised institution. The Budapest Treaty ensures that an applicant, i.e. a person who applies for a patent, needs not to deposit the biological material in all countries where he/she wants to obtain a patent. The applicant needs only to deposit the biological material at one recognised institution, and this deposit will be recognised in all countries party to the Budapest Treaty.

International Depositary Authority (IDA):

The deposits are made at an International Depositary Authority (IDA) in accordance with the rules of the Treaty on or before the filing date of the complete patent application. Article 7 of the Budapest treaty outlines the requirements for a facility to become an International Depositary Authority. As of March 1, 2008, there were 37 IDAs in approximately 20 countries worldwide.

Depositable Subject Matter:

IDA's have accepted deposits for biological materials which do not fall within a literal interpretation of "microorganism." The Treaty does not define what is meant by "microorganism." Microorganisms that are naturally occurring cannot be the subject of patents. However, a naturally occurring microorganism that is manipulated or altered such as through gene insertion, mutation etc can be the subject of a patent.

Patent law requires that the details of an invention must be fully disclosed in order for others skilled in the relevant field to be able to replicate it. Disclosure is normally achieved by means of a written description and supplemented where necessary by drawings. In the case of inventions involving the use of microorganisms, these patentability requirements may be difficult to fulfill.

EXAMPLE: It would be almost impossible to describe an organism isolated from soil and improved by selection, e.g. mutation, so that another person could be guaranteed to isolate and improve exactly the same strain from the soil in exactly the same way.

To overcome these problems, intellectual property offices in many countries recommended that the written description of an invention involving the use of a new microorganism be supplemented by the deposit of the microorganism in a recognized culture collection. The Budapest Treaty on the International Recognition of the Deposit of Microorganisms for the Purposes of Patent Procedure was introduced in 1980 in an effort to implement such recommendations. The Budapest Treaty recognizes 'international' depositary authorities for microorganisms, sets out the minimum standards for such collecting authorities, and also sets out the guidelines for the deposit of microorganisms. This treaty enables the deposit of the microorganism to help to satisfy the patentability requirements and also ensures that the microorganism is fully disclosed to the public.

The term "microorganism" is not defined in the Treaty. Whether a particular deposit is a microorganism or not matters less than whether the deposit is necessary for the purposes of disclosure. Tissue culture and nucleic acid molecules e.g. plasmids, can be deposited under the Treaty, even though they are not strictly microorganisms.

The range of materials able to be deposited under the Budapest Treaty includes:

- cells, for example, bacteria, fungi, eucaryotic cell lines, plant spores;
- genetic vectors (such as plasmids or bacteriophage vectors or viruses) containing a gene or DNA fragments;
- organisms used for expression of a gene (making the protein from the DNA).

There are many types of expression systems: bacterial; yeast; viral; plant or animal cell cultures;

- yeast, algae, protozoa, eucaryotic cells, cell lines, hybridomas, viruses, plant tissue cells, spores, and hosts containing materials such as vectors, cell organelles, plasmids, DNA, RNA, genes and chromosomes;
- purified nucleic acids; or
- deposits of materials not readily classifiable as microorganisms, such as "naked" DNA, RNA, or plasmids

Under the Treaty, certain culture collections are recognized as "International Depositary Authorities" (IDA) and a deposit made in the IDA is recognized by all Contracting States to the Treaty. The microorganisms that are deposited with the IDA are kept for a period of at least thirty years or five years after the most recent request for a sample (whichever is longer). The Treaty does not specify at which point during the patenting process the sample must be deposited by the inventor; this is governed by national law. National laws also govern the conditions under which the samples can be accessed by other interested parties.

INDIAN PATENT ACT, 1970 and AMENDMENTS:

A patent is a monopoly right granted to a person who has invented a new and useful article or a new process of making an article. The first provision in the nature of patent rights in India, which was at that time under the British Rule, was enacted in 1856. Under this act, the monopolies were styled "exclusive privileges." This act was replaced into 1857 as it was introduced without the previous sanction of the Queen. Soon after that in 1859, another act free from the defects of 1857 was passed. In 1872, the provisions of the Act of 1859 were further added by the provisions of "the Patents of Designs Protection Act," which solely related to designs.

The Act of 1872 was further supplemented in 1883 and it again revised and replaced by the "Indian Patents and Designs Act, 1911." This was amended from time to time in 1920, 1930, 1945, before the declaration of independence to India.

Based on the interim report the previous act was modified, regarding working of the invention in 1952 and in 1953 the Controller was authorized to grant licenses on foods, medicines, etc. Based on the final report, which was, in turn, based on the UK Patents Act, 1949, a Bill was introduced in the parliament in 1953 but the same could not be passed. The then judge, Justice (Retd.) N. Raja Gopala Ayyanger was requested to advise the government regarding the revision of the law. He submitted the report in 1959. Based on his report and also the report of the Joint Committee of the Parliament, the Patents Act, 1970 was passed in February 1972.

The Patents Act, 1970 is a landmark in the industrial development of India. The basic philosophy of the Act is that patents are granted to encourage inventions and to ensure that these inventions are worked on commercial skills without undue delay. Patents are not granted merely to enable patentee to enjoy a monopoly for the importation of the patented article into the country. It may be noted that the products vital for our economy such as agriculture and horticulture products, atomic energy inventions and all living things are not patentable. Thus, the Patents Act 1970 provided a reasonable balance between adequate and effective protection of patents on the one hand and the technology development, public interest and specific needs of the country on the other hand. However, the Patents Act, 1970 was criticized by the industrialized countries for having only process patents and not product patents in certain areas like foods, medicines/drugs and chemical sectors and short term of patent i.e., 7 to 14 years*.

*[*Under Indian Law the Term of Patents is not the same for all kinds of inventions. In respect of process, patents relating to drugs 7, foods the term is 5 yrs. from the date of sealing of patents or 7 yrs. from the date of patents whichever is shorter. In respect of all other patents, the term is 14 yr. from the date of patent. A patent has to be kept alive only by paying renewal fee from time to time.*]

Being the signatory to TRIPS agreement, India was put under the contractual obligation to amend its Patents Act in compliance with the provisions of TRIPS. India had to meet the first requirement on 1.1.1995. This was to give a pipeline protection till the country start giving product patents. However, the amendment could be passed only in 1999 [i.e., the Patent (Amendment) Act, 1999] and it came into force on 26th March 1999 retrospective from 1.1.1995. It laid down the provisions for filing of application for product patents in the field of drugs and agrochemicals with effect from 01.01.1995 as Mail Box applications and introduced the grant of exclusive marketing rights on those products.

PATENTS AMENDMENTS 1999:

TRIPS Agreement provides that patents shall be available for any invention whether products or processes, in all fields of technology (ART. 27). A transition period of 5 years is offered to all developing countries to make their laws compatible with the TRIPS Agreement. Moreover the countries that do not provide for product patents in certain areas can avail of further period of five years for amending their laws to provide for product patents. India does not grant product patents for food, drugs, pharmaceuticals and products produced by chemical process.

The Patents Amendment Act 1999 was passed in March 1999 to confirm with these international obligations and has retrospective effect from 1st January 1995. The main features of the amendments are as follows:

[I] Section 5 (2) has been inserted by this amendment which provides for filing of applications for patent of a product in the field of drugs, medicines and agro-chemicals. It also includes alloys, optical glass, semi-conductors and inter-mechanic compounds. These applications are kept pending till the law is suitably amended.

[II] Exclusive Marketing Rights (EMR):-

As per the TRIPS agreement, India has provided for EMR as a pipeline protection for pharmaceutical and agro-chemical products. EMR constitutes a monopoly right given to the patent applicant even before the grant of a patent. It is a right conferred upon the applicant to distribute and market his product in India without the same having been subjected to examination by applying the test and criteria for grant of a patent.

To be eligible for EMR the following conditions are to be fulfilled:

1) The applicant will have to file an application in India containing claims for products. Theses applications are kept in the "Mail Box" i.e. no action is taken on them.

2) File application and obtain a patent for identical invention in a member country.

3) Obtain marketing approval from the same convention country.

4) Obtain marketing approval from the appropriate authority in India; and

5) Then file an application to the controller of patents for the grant of EMR in India.

In case of inventions made in India, the applicant does not have to obtain product patent and marketing approvals from some other member country but has an option to have his process patent for identical invention obtained in India.

Also, EMR is not available for products for which applications have been made before 1.1. 1995 Exclusive Marketing Rights is only for selling and distributing the product but not for manufacturing the same and is granted for five years from the date of the EMR application or till the patent is granted on his mail box application, or his patent application is rejected whichever is earlier. Amendments have also been made to protect the public interest. EMR is available only till 31–12–2004

[III] An applicant in India can file an application for a patent outside India simultaneously while filing the same in India. Earlier the applicant was required to file such application only after the expiry of six weeks after the date on which the application was filed in India.

[IV] The present amendment also provides for the protection of security of India. According to the provisions the Central Government shall not disclose any information relating to any patentable invention or any application relating to the grant of patent under this Act, which it considers prejudicial to the interest of security of India. It shall take action including the revocation of any patent, which it considers necessary in the interest of security of India. This provision is universally found in the Patent Legislation.

[V] Further the Patent Rules have been modified to make them simpler. These rules have made the forms simpler, thus facilitating convenience and speed.

[VI] Patent Co-operation Treaty (PCT): India has joined the Paris Convention. Eventually it has become a member of PCT.

Chapter II (A) has been inserted in the Indian Patent Rules, by way of this amendment. This chapter deals with International Applications under PCT. PCT provides for filing of an international applications where protection is sought in different countries. Filing of such an application has the same effect as if the application had been filed separately in each of the countries in which protection is desired. The Indian Patent Office has been designated as the receiving office for PCT applications.]

India amended its Patent Act again in 2002 to meet with the second set of obligations (Term of Patent, etc.), which had to be effected from 01.01.2000. This amendment has the provisions for 20 years term for the patent, reversal of burden of proof, etc., came into force on 20th May 2003 along with Patent Rules 1972. The third amendment to the Patent Act, 1970 made to incorporate the provisions for granting product patents based on the obligations to be fulfilled as on 01.01.2005 has already been brought into force by the Patents (Amendments) Act, 2005 and Patents (Amendment) Rules 2005.

[*There are **four Schedules** to the Patents (Amendment) Rules, 2005:*

First Schedule*: it prescribe the fees to be paid,*

Second Schedule*: specifies the list of forms and the texts of various forms of required in connection with various activities under the Patents Act. These forms are to be used wherever required and, if needed, can be modified with the consent of the Controller.*

Third Schedule*: prescribes the form of Patent to be issued on Grant of the Patent.*

Fourth Schedule*: prescribes costs to be awarded in various proceedings before the Controller under the Act.*]

The Patent (Amendment) Rules, 2006, with a view to ensure time bound disposal of patent applications, has prescribed definitive time frames for various activities by the Patent Offices.

The Patent (Amendment) Rules, 2006: *with a view to ensure time bound disposal of patent applications, has prescribed definitive time frames for various activities by the Patent Offices.*

A patent application now has to be referred to an Examiner within one month of a request for its examination. Further, the Controller will now be required to take a decision on the report of the Examiner within one 1month of its submission and the First Examination Report has also to be issued within six months of the date of request for examination of a patent application. The time for granting permission to file patents abroad has also been reduced from 3 months to just 21 days.

Patent applications are now to be compulsorily published within one month after expiry of the statutory period of 18 months and, in case of request for an early publication, the application is to be published within one month from the date of request. This step will introduce an element of certainty regarding the date of publication, which was previously not available.

Further the timelines available for applicants and the public have also been extended. Accordingly the time frame for:

1. *Making a request for examination has been extended from 36 to 48 months.*

2. *Filing a pre-grant opposition extended from 3 to 6 months.*

3. *Filing reply to pre-grant opposition extended from 1 to 3 months.*

4. *Meeting the requirements of the First Examination Report increased from 6 to 12 months.*

Changes have also been made to make the patent rules user-friendly.

1. *The working of the Patent Offices has also been decentralized completely. All patent activities can now be carried on by all the patent offices (Delhi, Mumbai, Kolkata & Chennai). Earlier certain patent activities could be carried out only by the Head Office (Patent Office at Kolkata).*

2. *Fees to the Patent Office can now be paid electronically.*

RULES BEFORE AMENDMENTS	RULES AFTER AMENDMENTS
1. Request for examination to be made within **36 months** from date of priority or from date of filing application.	Request for examination to be made within **48 months** from date of priority or from date of filing application.
2. Controller to refer the application to Examiner	Controller to refer the application to Examiner within **1 month from date of publication or 1 month from request for examination** whichever is later.
3. Meeting the requirements of the First Examination Report – **6 months** from the date of issue of the report.	Meeting the requirements of the First Examination Report – **12 months** from date of issue of the report.
4. A pre-grant opposition to be filed within **3 months** from the date of publication for the application or before the grant of patent.	A pre-grant opposition to be filed within **6 months** from the date of publication of the application or before the grant of patent.
5. Reply to pre-grant opposition to be filed within **1 month** from date of notice of opposition.	Reply to pre-grant opposition to be filed within **3 months** from date of notice of opposition.
6. Official fees to be paid in **cash or bank draft or cheque.**	Official fees to be paid in **cash or bank draft or cheque or electronically**.
7. Controller to decide on request for permission to file for patents abroad – **3 months** from date of request.	Controller to decide on request for permission to file for patents abroad - **21 days** from date of request.

The Patent System in India is governed by the Patents Act, 1970 as amended by the Patents (Amendments) Act, 2005 and the Patents Rules, 2003; as amended by Patents (Amendment) Rules 2006 effective from 05.05.2006.

The history of Patent legislations in India chronologically given as in table below:

1856	The Act VI of 1856 on protection of inventions based on the British Patent Law offered certain exclusive privileges granted to inventions of new manufactures for a period of 14 years
1859	The Act modified as Act XV, patent monopolies called Exclusive privileges
1872	The Patents and Designs Protection Act
1883	The Protection of Inventions Act
1888	Consolidated as Inventions Act
1911	The Indian Patents and Designs Act
1970	The Patents Act
1972	The Patents Act (Act 39 of 1970) came into force on 20th April 1972
1999	A bill of comprehensive amendment of Patents Act, 1970 was introduced in Lok Sabha

2002   The above bill was passed on 8th May, 2002 as Patents (Amendment) Act and came into force on 20th May 2003

2005   The Patents Act, 1970 as amended by the Patents (Amendments) Act, 2005 along with the Patents (Amendments) Rules, 2005 (w.e.f 1st January 2005)

2006   The Patent (Amendment) Rules, 2006, with a view to ensure time bound disposal of patent applications, has prescribed definitive time frames for various activities by the Patent Offices (with effect from 05.05.2006)

Salient features of Indian Patents Law (since 1.1.2005):

a) The Indian Patents law is now fully TRIPS Compatible.

b) Both Product as well as Process Patent available in all sectors including pharmaceuticals.

c) The term for both Product as well as Process Patent is now 20 years.

d) During the interim period 1995–2005, there were provisions for Exclusive Marketing Rights (EMRs). Simultaneously, the patent applications were kept in the Mail Box. The number of patent applications filed in the Mail Box was over 7000. The Mail Box was opened after 1.1.2005 gradually and applications processed and patents granted or rejected on merits.

e) The Pre-Grant Opposition as provided under 1970 Act was retained to a slightly reduced extent. Needless to say revocation of patent after grant (Post-Grant Opposition) was also retained as such.

f) Compulsory licensing Chapter was re-drafted in light of the Doha Declaration of 2001. The main changes brought in were National Health Policy to get precedence over IPR rights.

g) The Third Amendment passed in 2005 also gave powers to member countries of WTO to override the compulsory licence provisions under health emergencies and also empowered the States to supply essential medicines to other countries facing health emergency.

h) The Second Amendment passed in the year 2002 incorporated the Patent Cooperation Treaty (PCT) passed by World Intellectual Property Organization (WIPO) earlier. This provided for international patenting and enforcement.

i) One of the most important changes made (passed by the Third Amendment in 2005) was to define 'Patentability Criteria' in the light of Doha Declaration. It made "minor improvements" (improvements which could not be considered to have significant therapeutic advancement) non-patentable.

As TRIPS deals with all IPRs, as many as 8 legislations were amended or freshly enacted to bring in full TRIPS compatibility in all other IPRs. The law relating to Trade Marks and Copyrights was amended. New legislations were passed for Farmers and Breeders' Rights and Bio-diversity.

Indian Bio-Diversity Act 2002:

In order to protect the interest of our indigenous communities and their 'Indigenous' (IK) previously called 'Traditional Knowledge' TK); and also to enable them to share the gains from commercialization of our 'IK," India enacted Indian Bio-Diversity Act 2002. This incorporates and consolidates the law on this subject and follows the international agreement on Biodiversity i.e. UPOV (1992). However, there is one lacuna which has not been plugged as yet. Under the TRIPS Agreement as also under WIPO's PLT and

SPLT, the subject relating to "Indigenous" (traditional) knowledge has not been covered. Therefore, while applying for a patent in developed countries, it is not mandatory to disclose the source and geographical origin of biological material. It may be noted that this is a primary requirement as far as the Indian Patents Act is concerned (Section 10). However, since it is not so provided in the TRIPS Agreement, the developed countries have avoided and are opposing making it manda tory. The demand from developing countries is that such disclosure should be made mandatory, without which a patent application should not be accepted. This subject is being debated both in TRIPS as well as in WIPO and requires an amendment of the TRIPS Agreement.

Traditional Knowledge – Digital Library (TKDL):

On the promulgation of the TRIPS regime, there were widespread apprehensions in developing countries particularly India, that their traditional knowledge might be stolen and patented by the developed countries. This had actually happened in the case of Turmeric and Neem upon which India successfully contested the patent granted by the America and EU patent offices. In order to prevent recurrence of such cases, CSIR has established a digital library relating to Indian Ayurvedic and herbal medicines and plants. This is one of our biggest efforts to protect our TK.

TRIPS compatibility of Indian Patent Laws:

We have earlier referred to the transition period of 10 years which India got to bring its IP laws in line with the TRIPS Agreement. This was done through three amendments to the Indian Patents Act 1970:

1) First Amendment – 1999: Introduced Exclusive Marketing Rights (EMRs) for post 1995 inventions. This was a sort of temporary patent of 5 years till their patent applications (simultaneously filed and kept in the Mail Box), could be processed. The Mail Box which was to be opened after 01.01.2005 has been opened. Most of the patent applications under the Mail Box have been scrutinized and decided (over 7000 applications from Pharmaceutical sector).

2) Second Amendment – 2002: The Patents Act 1970 was made TRIPS compatible. Several changes were made with regard to Patentability, Application, Examination, Publication, Pre-Grant Opposition, Compulsory Licensing, etc. Pre-Grant Opposition provisions were retained at a slightly reduced level. Licence of right provision was abolished being non-compatible with TRIPS.

3) Third Amendment – 2005: Full TRIPS compatibility. The Product Patent Regime comes in force from 1.1.2005. Several changes in light of the Doha Declaration on public health were made - most important among them were - Section 3 (d) which denies patentability to minor improvements, enhanced governmental powers in health emergencies, enhanced governmental powers to allow export of urgently needed drugs to countries which did not have the capability of producing them etc.

WIPO-Administered Treaties:

Following are the 24 treaties administered by WIPO including the WIPO Convention.

IP Protection	Global Protection System	Classification
Berne Convention	Budapest Treaty	Locarno Agreement
Brussels Convention	Hague Agreement	Nice Agreement
Madrid Agreement (Indications of Source)	Lisbon Agreement	Strasbourg Agreement

IP Protection	Global Protection System	Classification
Nairobi Treaty	Madrid Agreement (Marks)	Vienna
Paris Convention	Madrid Protocol	
Patent Law Treaty	PCT	
Phonograms Convention		
Rome Convention		
Singapore Treaty on the Law of Trademarks		
Trademark Law Treaty		
Washington Treaty		
WCT		
WPPT		

Case studies

5

5.1: Turmeric Patent Case

Two US based Indians Suman K Das and Hari Har P. Cohly were granted a US Patent 5,40,504 on March 28, 1995 on "Use of Turmeric in wound healing." The patent was assigned to University of Mississippi Medical Center, USA. This patent claimed the administration of an effective amount of turmeric through local and oral route to enhance the wound healing process, as a novel finding. Any patent, before it is granted has to fulfill the basic requirements of novelty, non-obviousness and utility. Thus, if the claims have been covered by relevant published art, then the patent becomes invalid. CSIR could locate 32 references (some of them being more than one hundred years old and in Sanskrit, Urdu and Hindi), which showed that this finding was well known in India prior to filing of this patent. The formal request for re-examination of the patent was filed by CSIR at USPTO on 28th October 1996.

The first office action in the re-examination was issued by USPTO on 28th March, 1997, which rejected all the six claims based on the references submitted by CSIR as being 'anticipated by the submitted references' and therefore considered invalid under 35 U.S.C. 102 and 103. After receiving the first action, the University of Mississippi Medical Centre, to whom the turmeric patent was assigned, decided not to pursue the case and transferred the rights to the inventors, who, however, decided to file a response. The inventors argued that the powder and paste had different physical properties, i.e. bio-availability and absorbability, and therefore, one of ordinary skill in the art would not expect, with any reasonable degree of certainty, that a powdered material would be useful in the same application as a paste of the same material. The inventors, further, mentioned that oral administration was available only with honey and honey itself was considered to have wound healing properties.

In the second Office Action, the examiner rejected all the claims once again and made his action final. He made it clear that the paste and the powder forms were "equivalent" for healing wounds in view of the cited art. Subsequent to the second rejection, the inventors had an interview with the examiner and deleted claims 5 6 and also restricted the invention to a "non-healing surgical wound" as supported by the two case histories mentioned in the patent stating that there was no disclosure or suggestion of using turmeric in surgically inflicted non-healing wounds and requested the examiner to allow the amended claims. On 20th November 1997, the examiner rejected all the claims once again as being anticipated and obvious. The re-examination certificate was issued on this case on April 21, 1998 bringing the re-examination proceedings to a close.

The following points are interesting to note:

1. The turmeric case was a landmark case in that this was the first time that a patent based on the traditional knowledge of a developing country was challenged successfully and USPTO revoked the

patent. This eventually opened up the path to the creation of Traditional Knowledge Digital Library, Traditional Knowledge Resource Clarification, and finally inclusion of traditional knowledge in the International Patent Clarification System.

2. Amidst the loud protests against 'biopiracy' and 'theft' of India's biodiversity and traditional knowledge by foreign nationals, it is interesting to note here that the patentees were Indians (Das and Cohly), the re-examination in USPTO was done by an Indian (Kumar) and the re-examination was sought by an Indian institution (CSIR).

Source: (IPR and The Third world, by Dr. R.A. Mashelkar, Director General Council of Scientific and Industrial Research (CSIR))

5.2: Basmati Rice Case

Rice Tec Inc. had applied for registration of a mark "TEXMATI" before the UK Trade Mark Registry. It was successfully opposed by Agricultural and Processed Food Exports Authority (APEDA). One of the documents relied upon by Rice Tec as evidence in support of the registration of the said mark was the U.S. Patent 5,663,484 (hereafter referred to as '484 patent) granted by US Patent Office to Rice Tec on September 2, 1997 and that is how this patent became an issue for contest.

This US utility patent '484, was in a unique way to claim a rice plant having characteristics similar to the traditional Indian Basmati Rice lines and with the geographical delimitation covering North, Central or South America or Caribbean Islands. The patent was granted to Rice Tec by the U.S. Patent Office on September 2, 1997. The said patent covered 20 claims covering not only a novel rice plant but also various rice lines; resulting plants and grains, seed deposit claims, method for selecting a rice plant for breeding and propagation. Its claims 15–17 were for a rice grain having characteristics similar to those from Indian Basmati rice lines. The said claims 15–17 would have come in the way of Indian exports to US, if legally enforced. The grant of this patent created a stir in the public, government, business circles and academics.

In the wake of this controversy, the Government of India set up a Task Force under the Chairmanship of Secretary, Ministry of Industrial Development, to examine the possibilities of filing a re-examination request against the above mentioned US Patent. The Task Force, in turn, set up a Technical Committee comprising primarily the ICAR & CSIR scientists to examine the Patent specification in detail and to collect necessary documentary evidence that may be required to file the re-examination request against the US Patent.

Evidence from the IARI Bulletin was used against claims 15–17. The evidence was backed up by the germplasm collection of Directorate of Rice Research, Hyderabad since 1978. The various grain characteristics were evaluated by CFTRI scientists and accordingly the claims 15–17 were attacked on the basis of the declarations submitted by CFTRI scientists on grain characteristics.

Eventually, a request for re-examination of this patent was filed on April 28, 2000. Soon after filling the re-examination request, Rice Tec chose to withdraw claims 15 to 17 along with claim 4.

Although RiceTec did withdraw these claims, the US Patent Office on its own judged that 'a substantial question of patentability has been raised in respect of the remaining claims.

Based the exhaustive office action, Ricetec has now surrendered the claims 1 to 3, 5 to 7, 10, 14 and 18 to 20.

As such, the claims that Ricetec now intends to protect are 8,9,11,12 & 13. These claims pertain to specific rice lines and the progeny and the grains of the specific crosses. This means that as against the Indian attack on 3 claims, Ricetec is withdrawing 15 claim.

In summary, Ricetec having withdrawn claims 15–17, the threat of infringement by the export of Basmati grains to US has been averted. And now, with the surrender of all the other broad claims, even the alleged threat to the export of grains of insensitive rice lines from India has been averted. In short, the objective for which India had filed the re-examination case has been fulfilled.

Source: (IPR and The Third world, by Dr. R.A. Mashelkar, Director General Council of Scientific and Industrial Research (CSIR))

5.3: Ginger Case

A patent specification titled "Pharmaceutical composition for the treatment of excess mucous production" was filed at British Patent Office having a patent priority date of March 16, 2006 by the inventor Nicholas John Larkins. The british patent application discloses a composition comprising ginkgo biloba or extract or component thereof; apocynin; and a gingerol. The composition may be used to treat diseases such as Cystic fibrosis (CF) and Chronic obstructive pulmonary disease (COPD).

The patent applicant found that compositions according to the invention may have a remarkable effect in reducing excessive mucous production, especially excessive pulmonary mucous production. Moreover, the use of a gingerol (or gingerols) in combination with ginkgo biloba (or extract or component thereof) and apocynin provided a substantial clinical improvement; and especially a substantial reduction in excessive mucous production. It is apparent that there is a synergistic clinical outcome when a gingerol (or gingerols) is added to a preparation comprising ginkgo biloba (or standardised extract or component thereof), and apocynin.

The important patent claims of the patent application are as follows:

1. A composition comprising ginkgo biloba or extract or component thereof; apocynin; and a gingerol.

2. A composition according to claim 1 wherein the gingerol is in the form of a natural gingerol.

3. A composition according to claim 1 or claim 2 wherein the gingerol is in the form of Zingiber Officinale.

5. A composition according to any preceding claim comprising gingerol in the form of isolated gingerol.

23. A method of treatment or amelioration of disease by reduction of excessive mucous production comprising the step(s) of administering to the subject a composition comprising ginkgo biloba, or extract or component thereof; apocynin; and a gingerol.

However, Zingiber Officinale is the scientific name for ginger and commonly known as adrak in India. Ginger has been used as medicinal remedy for cough and cold since ages in India. Moreover, the medicinal properties of ginger has been the traditional knowledge of India. Consequently, the department of AYUSH and Council of Scientific and Industrial Research (CSIR) as stated by timeofindia newspaper intervened and provided evidence from age-old ayurveda and unani books, dating back to the 18th century that talked about ginger to treat cough and other diseases.

Patent prior art knowledge was retrieved from the Traditional Knowledge Digital Library (TKDL) database of India and submitted at the UK patent office. Subsequently, the patent examiner took into consideration of the prior art traditional knowledge of India and rejected the patent application for the ginger based pharmaceutical composition for the treatment of excess mucous production.

Currently, the Traditional Knowledge Digital Library (TKDL) database provides access to 2.23 Lakh medicinal formulations which were available in Indian ancient books. The Traditional Knowledge Digital Library (TKDL) database is available to Patent Offices across globe only under TKDL Access Agreement.

Source: https://biotechpatentattorney.wordpress.com/

5.4: Bajaj Auto Limited vs. TVS Motor Company Limited Case

Dispute over Patent for the Use of Twin-Spark Plug Engine Technology

Bajaj's patent:

According to the Bajaj Auto Limited (hereinafter the appellant), it was granted Indian Patent No. 195904 in respect of a patent application titled "An Improved Internal combustion engine working on four stroke principle" with a priority date of 16th July2002. The patent was granted on 7th July, 2005.Features of the invention are:a.Small displacement engine as reflected by

a) cylinder bore diameter between 45 mm and 70 mm.

b) Combustion of lean air fuel mixtures;

c) Using a pair of spark plugs to ignite the air fuel mixture at a predetermined instant In the patent, the invention by the applicants called "DTS-i Technology" was relating to the use of twin spark plugs for efficient combustion of lean air fuel mixture in small bore ranging from 45 mm to 70 mm internal combustion engine working on 4stroke principle.

TVS launches FLAME- the Bone of Contention:

The Respondents, M/s. TVS Motor Company Limited announced to launch motor bikes of 125-CC on 14th December 2007 under the trade mark 'FLAME.' Themotorcycle was powered with a lean burn internal combustion engine of bore size 54.5 mm with a twin spark plug configuration, which according to the Bajaj AutoLtd., infringes its patent. Therefore, before the launch of motor bikes, the applicantshave brought the suit before the court to protect their intellectual property

TVS files suit under section 105 and 106 of the Patents Act, 1970:

In October, 2007, the respondent filed the suit (C.S. No. 979 of 2007) before theMadras High Court under Sections 105 and 106 of the Patents Act, 1970 alleging thatthe statement made by the applicant on 1st and 3rd September, 2007 constituted agroundless threat.They learnt that the respondent has also filed a suit for defamation against theapplicant in the Bombay High Court.

Application for revocation of the applicant's patent:

The applicant also came to know that only 7 days before the launch of the proposed125-CC motorcycle, the respondent filed an application for revocation of applicant's patent No. 195904 before Indian Patents Appellate Board ("IPAB") under Section 64 of the Patents Act, 1970.

Launch of the disputed bike:

As opposed to the expectations of the applicants, the respondents later in the month of December of 2007, launched the bikes without making any change into that.

DECISION OF THE COURT

After considering the pleadings and various facets of the case, the learned single judgeheld that the concepts of prima facie case, balance of convenience and inadequacy of damages was in favour of the applicant. The grant of injunction was in favour of theapplicant.Thus, the interim injunction was granted in favour of the applicant.

(Intellectual Property & Information Technology Laws News Bulletin,2010)

5.5: The Coca-Cola Company vs. Bisleri International Pvt. Ltd Case

IPR Law- Infringement: Export: Threats: Jurisdiction – The Delhi High Court held that if the threat of infringement exists, then this court would certainly have jurisdiction to entertain the suit.

It was also held that the exporting of goods from a country is to be considered as sale within the country from where the goods are exported and the same amounts to infringement of trade mark.

In the present matter, the defendant, by a master agreement, had sold and assigned the trade mark MAAZA including formulation rights, know-how, intellectual property rights, goodwill etc for India only. with respect to a mango fruit drink known as MAAZA.

In 2008, the defendant filed an application for registration of the trade mark MAAZA in Turkey started exporting fruit drink under the trade mark MAAZA. The defendant sent a legal notice repudiating the agreement between the plaintiff and the defendant, leading to the present case. The plaintiff, the Coca Cola Company also claimed permanent injunction and damages for infringement of trade mark and passing off.

It was held by the court that the intention to use the trade mark besides direct or indirect use of the trade mark was sufficient to give jurisdiction to the court to decide on the issue. The court finally granted an interim injunction against the defendant (Bisleri) from using the trade mark MAAZA in India as well as for export market, which was held to be infringement of trade mark.

5.6: Apple vs Samsung Case

Apple Inc. is an American multinational, was founded by Steve Jobs in April 1st 1976, and has head office in Cupertino, California USA. Apple is well known for personal computers, Mobiles, electronics and its software. Most famous product of Apple is iPhone (Mobile), iPod (Portable music player), iPad (Tablets), Mac Book Air (Personal computers), OS X and iOS (operating system). It has presence in hardware, software and electronics.

Apple is 2nd largest IT Company in terms of revenue and 3rd largest mobile maker company in the world. Apple has doing lot of R & D on its product to come in market. Apple registered a lot of patents for design, software and its technologies in USA and all over the world.

Defendants

Samsung Group is a South Korean multinational company, founded by Lee Byung Chul in 1938, and has head office in Samsung town, Seoul, South Korea. It is Electronics, Electronics components, Semiconductors, Medical Device Company. It is very famous for mobiles and semiconductor chip. Galaxy series of mobile phones and Galaxy Tab are very popular products in all over the world. Samsung is number 1 IT company and number 1 in mobile phone maker Company in all over the world. Samsung also has lot of patented technologies in mobile and wireless technology area.

Samsung supply ARM processor to Apple which is used in every iPad and iPhone. Samsung is ahead of Apple in term of revenue, rank and market share.

Detail of Case

Apple launched iPhone mobile phone in 2007, which was small and lightweight sophisticated device with some unique and patented interface and technology. In same year it launched iPod, a portable music player. In 2010 Apple launched iPad Tablets, an advanced version of iPhone, a category have capacity to replace computers. Its entire product got a lot of prize in all over the world and best selling. During 2007 to 2010 Apple exceeded revenue to US $ 2 billion.

Samsung launched Galaxy S in 2010, a mobile phone based on Google's operating system Android. It also launched Galaxy S2 and Galaxy Tab in 2011. Selling of these products was increasing and it stood before Apple for competition.

In April 15, 2011 Apple filed complaint against Samsung for its Android phone and tablets in district court of California. Apple's complain was that Samsung's products are infringing intellectual property of its flagship product.

Apple said that Samsung infringing its patent, trademark and user interface and style.

Apple included following product of Samsung initially

Nexus S, Galaxy S 4G, Epic 4G, Galaxy Tab

Apple submitted comparison of iPhone 3G and Galaxy S to the court and charging for Patent infringement

False designation of origin Unfair competition Trademark Infringement etc.

Apple sued Samsung in many other countries for infringement. Samsung also sued Apple in Seoul, Tokyo, Germany and USA in April-June 2011.

In USA Samsung was charged for design and technology patent, Trade Dress and trademark violation by Apple. And in other company for technology patent and trademark violation.

Technology in Question

Apple's Utility Patent

Multi Touch user interface

Performing wide variety of function by user gesture like pinching, zooming, selecting and scrolling.

System for rearranging text messages and Bounce back feature.

These patents are US7812828, 7669134, 6493002, 7853891 etc.

Apple's Design Patent

Apple' unique design flat black face, metallic bezel, rounded corner etc.

These patents are D627790, 602016, and 618677.

Apple's Trade Dress

Protection for appealing and packing style of product.

Apple's packing style of iPhone and iPad.

Trade dress registration number 3470983, 3457218, 3475327 etc.

Trademark

Different icon of mobile phone and tab, like

Message icon,

Setting icon,

Music icon

Gallery icon etc.

Patentee's Arguments

1. Apple's said Samsung intentionally copy iPhone and iPad design and technology and launch imitate product in market.

2. False impression on consumer's mind.

3. Unfair competition by Samsung to downgrade its product.

4. Apple want injunction over Samsung's product.

5. Apple want damages which was around more than US $ 2 billion from Samsung.

Defendant's Arguments

1. Samsung develop its own product not imitate Apple's product.

2. Samsung use different trademark than Apple, differences are therein.

3. Samsung did market research to innovate product.

4. Samsung was claiming that Injunction is invalid.

Litigation

USA

Prove case of patent infringement (design, technology) and Trade Dress.

Fined appox US $ 1.5 billion on Samsung.

UK

Court denied case of Apple.

Product is not similar to Apple.

Germany

Ban on Galaxy Tab, infringing patent of Apple.

Consider only few violations.

Views

Apple got patented its lot of technology for mobile and tab. It sued to Samsung for infringing design, technology and Trade Dress. Samsung violate some patents like scrolling, bounce back etc. Apple and Samsung both are leader of market, they don't need to copy each other. Samsung violate patent but not intentionally, they did research in same area and innovate same technology.

Model Questions

1. Write a note on invention and creativity and distinguish between them.

2. Define invention. What are the statutory classifications of invention?

3. Distinguish between invention and innovation. Bring out the major reasons why the companies seriously involve in innovation.

4. What are the major steps involved in creative and inventive process.

5. What is Property? Explain briefly the general classifications of property.

6. What is an Intellectual Property? Explain the importance and need for the protection of intellectual Property.

7. Define Intellectual Property Rights (IPRs). What are the areas related to Intellectual Property as established by WIPO?

8. What do you mean by Intellectual Property Rights (IPRs)? Explain the basic forms of Intellectual Property Rights?

9. Write a note on

    a) Traditional Knowledge (TK)

    b) Geographical Indications (GI)

10. Explain briefly the concept of Copyrights and Neighbouring rights.

11. Write a note on GATT agreement and its relevance to Intellctual Property Rights.

12. What are the major rounds of GATT agreements and explain how they are important in dealing with international trade tariffs and settlement of trade disputes.

13. What are the major objectives of WTO?

14. Explain briefly the administrative mechanism of World Trade Organization.

15. Explain briefly the dispute settlement mechanism under WTO.

16. What do you mean by Dumping in international trade? What are the anti-dumping measures introduced by the WTO to ensure a fair trade relation among the member countries.

17. What are the major functions of World Trade Organization?

18. What are the WTO principles of trade policy? Explain.

19. Explain the position of India in WTO.

20. Substantiate the statement - "India – a raising power in WTO".

21. Explain briefly the features of TRIPS agreement.

22. What are the basic requirements of the TRIPS agreement? Explain.

23. Explain the provision for the protection of 'Computer Programs and Compilation of Data' under TRIPS agreement.

24. Explain briefly the role of TRIPS Council.

25. Does the TRIPS Agreement apply to all WTO members? Substantiate your answer.

26. Distinguish between Madrid Agreement and Madrid Protocol.

27. Write a note on India as a signatory to the Madrid Protocol on trademark protection.

28. Explain the role of Hague system in the protection of Industrial Design.

29. What are the qualifications stated to use the Hague System in seeking protection to Industrial Designs? Explain.

30. What are the strategic goals of WIPO?

31. Explain briefly the core activities of WIPO.

32. What is meant by 'Country of Origin' as stated in Berne Convention? Explain.

33. What do you mean by Moral Rights? Distinguish between 'right of paternity' and 'right of integrity.'

34. Write a note on 'DROIT DE SUITE.'

35. Explain briefly the provisions of the 'Paris Convention' on Industrial Property.

36. What are the major advantages of joining the Paris Convention? Explain.

37. Explain briefly the range of materials able to be deposited under the Budapest Treaty.

38. Write a note on Budapest Treaty.

39. Give a brief historical overview of Indian Patent Law.

40. Explain briefly the Indian Patent Act, 1970 and amendment thereon to make it TRIPS compatible.

41. What are the Salient features of Indian Patents Law after the enforcement of Indian Patent (Amendment) Act, 2005? Expalin.

42. What are the major amendments to the Indian Patent Act, 1970? Explain.

43. Define a Patent. Is patent a territorial right? Explain.

44. Why one should consider patenting the invention?

45. What is a Patent? Explain the need (importance) for a patent system.

46. What are the features of Patent Right? Explain.

47. If an invention is patentable, is it always wise to apply for patent protection? Evaluate.

48. What are the factors to be taken into consideration to decide on the feasibility of applying for patent right? Explain.

49. What are the conditions to be satisfied to ensure the patentability of an invention? Explain.

50. What is 'patentable subject matter?' Bring out the areas could be excluded from patentability.

51. Write a note on

    Employee Invention

    Independent Contractors

Joint Inventors

Joint Owners

52. What do you mean by 'First-to-file' and 'First-to-invent?' Explain.

53. Explain briefly the major types of patent application.

54. Write a note on:

Ordinary Application

Convention Application

PCT International Application

PCT National Phase Application

Application for Patent Addition

Divisional Application

55. What is a patent specification? Explain briefly the types of patent specification.

56. Write a note on Provisional Specification.

57. What is a Complete Specification? Explain the major parts (contents) of a complete specification.

58. Write a note on:

Prior Art

Patent Claims

59. What are the documents required for filing a patent application? Explain.

60. What is Patent Infringement? What are the relief in case of successful infringement proceedings? Explain.

61. What are the major steps or stages of patent procedure? Explain.

62. Explain briefly the grounds of opposition for the grant of patent?

63. Write a note on "Compulsory Licensing".

64. Explain briefly the PCT filing procedure.

65. What are the general precautions for applicant while patenting? Explain.

66. What do you mean by Patent Examination? Explain.

67. What are the contents of a patent application? Explain.

68. Explain the nature of the information needed while consulting a Patent Attorney.

69. Explain the time – frame of filing national patent application.

70. Explain briefly the method and time – frame of PCT patent filing procedure.

71. How a patentee can license his/her patent to others for commercial use? Explain.

72. Explain the three main ways (routes) of filing for patent protection abroad.

73. Write a note on 'Patenting Abroad.'

74. Write a note on Opposition to patent grant.

75. Explain briefly the case of 'Revocation of Turmeric Patent.'

76. Explain briefly the case of 'Revocation of Neem Patent.'

77. What is a Trademark? Explain briefly the characteristics of a Trademark.

78. What are the functions of Trademark? Explain.

79. Explain briefly the guidelines for the registration of Trademark.

80. What are the main reasons for rejecting an application for registration of trademarks? Explain.

81. What are the major categories of sings (marks) excluded from registration (not registrable)? Explain.

82. What are the non-traditional trademarks? Explain

83. Explain briefly the major types of Trademarks.

84. What are the major works protected and not protected by the Copyright? Explain.

85. What are the rights conferred by the Copyright? Explain.

86. What are the classifications of Software according to Copyright? Explain.

87. What is an Industrial Design? Explain its importance to a business organization.

88. What is the grace period? How long does Industrial Design protection last? Explain.

89. Define Industrial Design. What can be registered as an industrial design? Explain.

90. What cannot be protected by the Industrial Design rights? Explain.

91. How do you protect your Industrial Design abroad? Explain.

92. Why Ginger patent is revoked? Discuss.

93. What is the patent issue between Bajaj Auto Limited Vs. TVS Motor Company Limited?

94. There was a trademark issue between The Coca-Cola Company Vs. Bisleri International Pvt. Ltd, give a case study.

95. What was the patent for which Apple and Samsung were in front of court?

96. List out the arguments of Apple and Samsung company for their patent.

97. Give a brief account on emerging trends in IPR.

98. Describe Intellectual property Rights with Indian scenario.

99. What is the global scenario in the area of technology transfer?

100. How patenting system brings change in economic state of a country? Discuss.